Legends of
Texas Barbecue
Cookbook

Captain Will Wright of the Texas Rangers cooks his dinner over a campfire in the Chisos Mountains, circa 1930.

A barbecue stand made of corrugated tin, Corpus Christi, 1939.
photo by Russell Lee

LEGENDS OF TEXAS BARB

COOK

Recipes and

ROBB WALSH

ECUE

Recollections from the Pit Bosses

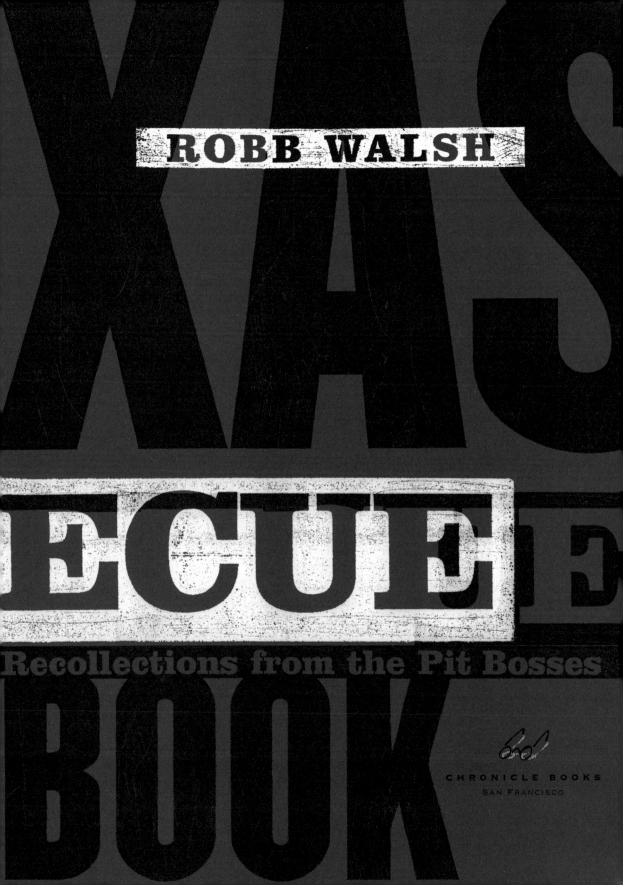

CHRONICLE BOOKS

SAN FRANCISCO

Library of Congress Cataloging-in-Publication Data:
Walsh, Robb.
    The Texas barbecue cookbook : recipes and recollections from the pit
bosses / by Robb Walsh.
        p. cm.
    ISBN 0-8118-2961-8 (pbk.)
    1. Barbecue cookery—Texas. 2. Barbecue cookery—Texas—
Anecdotes. I. Title.

    TX840.B3 W36 2002
    641.5'784'09764—dc21

2001047690

Manufactured in The United States of America.

Designed by Erin Mayes and DJ Stout, Pentagram, Austin
Diagrams by A.J. Garces

Distributed in Canada by Raincoast Books
9050 Shaughnessy Street
Vancouver, BC V6P 6E5

10 9 8 7 6 5 4

Chronicle Books LLC
85 Second Street
San Francisco, California 94105

www.chroniclebooks.com

Acknowledgments

THANKS TO BILL LEBLOND AT CHRONICLE BOOKS; AND ERIN MAYES AND DJ Stout at Pentagram, Austin for helping envision this project. And thanks to Katie and Julia Walsh for eating so much barbecue. And to Jay Francis for the help with testing recipes.

Thanks to all the pit bosses, cook-off competitors, and restaurant owners who took the time to talk to me and help me with recipes and advice, especially Vencil Mares, Harley Goerlitz, Marvin Lange, Tommy Wimberly, Rockney Terry, Bill Smolik, Louis Charles Henley, Brian Bracewell, Rick Schmidt, John Fullilove, James Drexler, Willie Mays, and Leon O'Neal.

Thanks to the outstanding photographers who have contributed to this book, especially Will Van Overbeek, Scott Van Osdol, and Wyatt McSpadden.

And thanks to my fellow Texas barbecue writers for all the inspiration, help, and goodwill, especially Bud Kennedy, June Naylor Rodriguez, Beverly Bundy, Jim Shahin, John Morthland, Pat Sharpe, Joe Nick Patoski, Richard Zelade, Dotty Griffith, Cathy Barber, and Kitty Crider. Thanks to Barbara Winters for helping put things together.

Many thanks also to the Taylor International Barbecue Cook-Off and to the entire fraternity of barbecue cook-off organizers, volunteers, judges, and competitors.

Barbecue fans owe a special debt of gratitude to the familes who maintain the Lone Star State's unique traditions, especially the Bracewell family, the Bryan family, the Drexler family, the Henley family, the Cotten family, the Novosad family, the Mays family, the Smolik family, the Schmidt family, the Mueller family, the Mikeska family, the Riscky family, and the Goode family. Their dedication to preserving the culinary culture and folklore of Texas is an inspiration to food lovers everywhere.

In memory of Phil Born

A far-flung family dynasty—
each of the four Mikeska brothers
built a barbecue restaurant in
a different Texas town.
Left to right: Jerry, Maurice,
Rudy (deceased), and Clem.
photo by Will Van Overbeek

The pit room door at Ruthie's in Navasota.

Introduction

TEXANS BARBECUE BEEF

THESE THREE WORDS ARE OFTEN USED TO SUM UP THE Texas barbecue experience. I understand why this knee-jerk explanation has become so popular: It reduces a long, complicated saga into a pat one-liner that no one can really disagree with. The true story of Texas barbecue is far more bewildering.

Southern barbecue is a proud thoroughbred whose bloodlines are easily traced. Texas barbecue is a feisty mutt with a whole lot of crazy relatives. The Southern barbecue style has remained largely unchanged over time. Texas barbecue is constantly evolving.

Before the Civil War, blacks on the plantations of East Texas, Hispanics in the Lower Rio Grande Valley, German immigrants in the Hill Country, and white subsistence farmers in the northeast corner of the state all had their own style of cooking meat. The meats were equally varied, including pork, mutton, goat, venison, squirrel, and any number of others. When the Texas cattle industry emerged after the war, beef became cheap and commonly available. Eventually it became a central part of everybody's cooking, but that's hardly the whole story.

Texans barbecue pork.

When visitors from Carolina and Tennessee come to Texas, they are generally astonished to find that we eat a lot of pork here as well as beef brisket. That's the problem with the beef generalization. Yes, we barbecue beef—but we're also fond of other meats. East Texas barbecue is a proud variant of the black Southern barbecue tradition, and while both consider pork their crowning glory, in East Texas they have their own way of doing things. Southern pork would never be served without barbecue sauce, but some East Texans like slow-smoked pork ribs with a little salt and pepper—and not a speck of sauce.

Texans barbecue sausage.

Now there's a Texas barbecue item you don't hear very much about. The concept of barbecued sausage seems to have originated in Texas's German belt in the 1800s. The smoked sausage produced by Czech and German meat markets in that part of the state would have been virtually indistinguishable from the smoked sausage that butchers produced in central Europe.

Who decided it was barbecue? It was most likely one of those accidents that occur when cultures bump into each other. Itinerant farm workers discovered the smoked meats in German butcher shops and, in the absence of any better explanation, they declared it to be barbecue. So it was.

And smoked sausage is still considered barbecue in every hamlet in the old German belt—from Smolik's in Cuero to City Market in Schulenburg to Dozier's Grocery in Fulshear. Little combination meat markets and barbecue joints crank out an endless variety of smoked sausages—links, rings, and uncut coils; garlic sausage; German sausage with mustard seed; all-pork sausage; all-beef sausage; sage sausage; Czech sausage with coarse black pepper; wet sausage; beef and pork sausage; and, of course, the perennial favorite, Elgin hot guts.

Texans barbecue cow heads.

This tradition traces its origins back to the Mexican barbacoa style, only it evolved into something completely different here. Now, you might say that a cow head cooked in an oven isn't really barbecue—but then you would have to define barbecue, which is always a tricky proposition.

Grilled shish kebab? Grilled salmon steaks? That's not barbecue in Texas—but smoked bologna is. They serve it at the Railhead in Fort Worth. Steaks on the gas grill? No way! But what if you cook a double-cut sirloin over mesquite coals in an enclosed pit? Sure! That's cowboy barbecue the way they do it at Cooper's in Llano—definitely a legitimate style of Texas barbecue.

Confused yet? Good. Because that's just the tip of the iceberg. I think it's fair to say that Texas has more variations in its barbecue styles than any other state. And more disagreements about them.

Truth be told, Texans barbecue all kinds of things in lots of different ways.

This book wasn't written to claim some kind of barbecue supremacy for Texas. Tennessee, the Carolinas, and other states have fine barbecue, and most Texans enjoy it when they visit those places. The intention of this book is to offer a broader view of what barbecue really means across the Lone Star State. And to give a little recognition to the African-Texans, Mexican-Texans, German-Texans, and Anglo cowboys and farmers whose culinary traditions have melded to form the cultural icon that is modern Texas barbecue.

I hope these recipes and tips preserve a little Texas folklore and also serve as an invitation to join in and barbecue Texas-style in your own backyard. Please enjoy this book exactly the way it was written—in the shade of a tall tree with the smoker going.

Women outside Louie Mueller's
Barbecue, Taylor, 1982.
photo by Michael Murphy

Roasting meats on the barbecue, circa 1900.

LEGENDARY BARBECUE

The Evolution of the Pit

Forty-two cattle were barbecued for a "Get Together" to bring farmers and townspeople together in Victoria, 1921.

THE PITMASTER SQUINTS INTO the smoke as he opens the giant steel door. From your place in line, you watch him fork and flip the juicy, black beef clods and sizzling pork loins. Your heart beats faster as he opens a steel door to reveal a dozen sausage rings hissing and spitting in the thick white cloud. Slowly, the sweet cloud of oak smoke makes its way to you, carrying with it the aroma of peppery beef, bacon-crisp pork, and juicy garlic sausage. Your mouth starts watering. You swallow hard. Your stomach rears back and lets out a growl. You're in a frenzy by the time you get to the head of the line, where the hot meats are being sliced and weighed. You order twice as much as you can eat. You carry it away on a sheet of butcher paper, with an extra sheet tucked underneath for a plate.

Welcome to Texas barbecue.

We love to eat it. We love to make it. And we love to argue about it. We have competing theories on the etymology, the definition of the word, and on those characteristics that make it uniquely Texan. We don't agree on the kind of wood, the need for sauce,

Pit boss Roy Perez at the old Kreuz Market in Lockhart, 1996.
photo by Wyatt McSpadden

Men in suits waiting for barbecued mutton cooking on an open pit, 1921.

the cut of meat, or which part of the state does it best. And we all have our favorite pit bosses. But we all agree that non-Texans don't understand it.

Traditional barbecue definitions don't make sense here. "Barbecue is always served with a distinctive sauce," say some. Not in Texas—some of our most famous barbecue joints serve no sauce at all. "Barbecue means slow cooking over the low heat of a wood or charcoal fire," say others. Sorry. Some of the best smoked meat in the Lone Star State is cooked at 600°F.

So what is Texas barbecue exactly?

If we can't quite agree on what it is, at least we can agree on where it came from. A look at the history of barbecue and the evolution of the modern barbecue pit explains a lot about our various styles.

If you include roasting meat on an open fire in your definition of barbecue, then the earliest Texans to barbecue were the Caddo Indians, who cooked venison and other game here ten thousand years ago. They were followed by the Spanish shepherds, who spit-roasted kid goat and lamb *al pastor* ("shepherd style") on the South Texas plains, starting in the 1600s.

The old Southern version of pit barbecue, meat cooked on a grate of sticks over hot coals in a hole in the ground, migrated to Texas from the South in several stages beginning in the early 1800s. Settlers used this open pit method to cook squirrels and venison. Mexican *barbacoa*, meat sealed in maguey leaves and buried in hot coals, has also been seen along the Rio Grande Valley for at least a hundred years.

Old World meat smoking was brought to Central Texas by German and Czech butchers during an era of intense European migration that began in the 1830s and reached its height around 1890. The German meat markets sold fresh meats and smoked their leftovers in enclosed smokers, as they had done in the Old Country. They were probably astonished when migrant farm workers began the tradition of eating that smoked meat on the spot. The old meat markets are now considered by some to be quintessential Texas barbecue joints, despite the fact that German smoked meats and sausages aren't really American barbecue.

When Texas entered the Union as a slave state in the 1850s, cotton planters from the Carolinas, Alabama, and Mississippi came to take advantage of the cheap land prices. Each plantation founder brought as many as a hundred slave families with him. When the slaves were freed in 1865, the African-American barbecue of East Texas became a style of its own.

According to *Eats: A Folk History of Texas Foods*, the first big civic

LEGENDS

Civic Barbecues

Big public barbecues were held for all kinds of reasons throughout Texas history. In fact, no civic celebration was complete without one.

1853 Stafford gave away free barbecue to the public to celebrate becoming a stop on the Buffalo Bayou, Brazos, and Colorado Railway.

1860 Sam Houston spoke at the "Great American Barbecue," a political rally thrown by the American Party in Austin. All citizens of the state were invited to attend and eat for free.

1891 The citizens of Whitney, a town with a declining population, held a barbecue to promote the benefits of citizenship. They gave away 3,500 pounds of barbecue.

1926 Edgar Byram Davis closed what was probably the biggest oil deal in the state up to that time. He got $12 million (half of it in cash) for his Luling oil holdings, and to celebrate he held a free barbecue. Attendance estimates run as high as thirty-five thousand.

1941 At his inauguration celebration, Governor W. Lee "Pappy" O'Daniel set up pits on the grounds of the capitol building in Austin and gave away barbecue to all comers. (Pictured above)

1964 President Lyndon Johnson hosted the president-elect of Mexico at a state dinner at the LBJ Ranch in Johnson City. Catered by Walter Jetton, this dinner for 250 is reported to be America's first official barbecue state dinner.

1991 The XIT ranch's annual reunion in Dalhart, cooked eleven thousand pounds of beef in pits dug with backhoes. The meat was served to twenty thousand guests.

Overhead view of the crowd at
W. "Pappy" Lee O'Daniel's 1941
inauguration party barbecue on
the grounds of the Texas Capitol.
The large circles are cowboy hats,
the smaller circles are plates.

Governor W. Lee "Pappy" O'Daniel applies mop sauce to meat being barbecued in an open pit on the capitol grounds, 1941.

barbecues began to be held around the state in the early 1800s. Pits were typically 25 feet long and 3 feet across. Whole sheep, goats, pigs, and steers were cut into pieces and cooked over oak or hickory coals while being continuously basted. The standard cooking time was twenty-four hours.

After the Civil War, beef became the meat most characteristic of Texas barbecue. In the days before refrigeration, barbecuing beef meant getting enough people together to make killing a whole steer worthwhile. When that happened it was quite a party. While the ultimate in Southern barbecue was cooking a whole hog, cooking a whole steer was the ultimate in Texas barbecue.

Because you could feed so many people with a whole steer, Texas barbecues started out big—and then they got bigger. Texans being Texans, barbecues became competitions, and each barbecue became an effort to outdo all others. This tradition lives on in such events as the XIT Annual Reunion in Dalhart, where tens of thousands of people gather year after year to attend the "world's largest free barbecue."

The Barbecue Barons

WALTER JETTON OF FORT WORTH WAS THE LAST OF the open pit barbecuers and probably the single most influential pit boss in Texas barbecue history. In the 1950s, Jetton held the record for barbecue catering, having fed twelve thousand people at one event. He also enjoyed considerable prestige as LBJ's favorite caterer. In 1965, Pocket Books published his *LBJ Barbecue Cookbook*.

Walter Jetton was a traditionalist and a purist. He dug pits in the ground, burned hardwood down to hot coals, and cooked meat directly over the coals for eighteen to twenty-four hours. Jetton dismissed modern barbecue equipment as claptrap. Unfortunately, cooking in a hole in the ground is frowned on by health inspectors these days.

County health departments regulate the use of barbecue pits in food service operations in Texas. The regulations, and how strictly they are enforced, have varied widely from county to county since the laws first hit the books during the health and sanitation crusades of the Progressive Era, in the early 1900s.

The brick smokers of German-belt meat markets offered a design model for other barbecue restaurants. Built over a hundred years ago, some of these pits still provide us with insights into how to set up a barbecue. Some barbecue joints, such as Green's in Houston and Novosad's in Halletsville, built cleverly designed pits with the cooking chamber indoors and the firebox outdoors.

Some cookbook authors have assumed that the pits in Texas barbecue restaurants were designed to

LEGENDS

Linguistic Lore

BQ

Some pretty fantastic etymologies for the word "barbecue" have been advanced over the years. Two cookbooks I've seen recount a tale about a wealthy Texas rancher who fed all his friends whole sheep, hogs, and cattle roasted over open pits. In one cookbook his name is Bernard Quayle, in the other it is Barnaby Quinn, but in both versions the branding iron of the ranch has his initials B. Q. with a straight line underneath. Texas ranches are named for their brands, and a straight line is called a bar. Thus, the "bar B.Q." became synonymous with fine eating— or so the story goes.

replicate the slow cooking over hot coals common in traditional pit barbecue. But that isn't always true. The heat of Kreuz's old smoker has been measured at temperatures as high as 600°F. When Texas barbecue moved from the hole in the ground to the restaurant kitchen, the smoking process was speeded up.

Mechanization

IN 1949, A HOUSTON MACHINIST named Leonard O'Neill won a tiny restaurant near Lenox Street in Houston in a game of craps. He renamed it the Lenox Barbecue, and by the 1960s the restaurant was catering for thousands of guests at a time, and O'Neill found himself competing head to head with the legendary Walter Jetton. In 1967, Ann Valentine, food editor of the *Houston Post*, wrote an article about the two mega-caterers titled "The Barbecue Barons."

Unlike Jetton, O'Neill prepared food at a restaurant, where he had to abide by the sanitary codes. But ordinary brick barbecue smokers couldn't accommodate jobs the size of those the Lenox Barbecue was being asked to do. So the former machinist introduced barbecue to the age of mechanization.

O'Neill bought an enormous bread-rising oven from the Rainbow Bread bakery. The oven had a rotating mechanism inside that moved the dough through a timed cycle. O'Neill converted this machinery into a mechanized wood smoke rotisserie that could cook three thousand pounds of meat at one time.

LEGENDS

Linguistic Lore
BABRACOT

According to the *Oxford English Dictionary,* the English word "barbecue" derives from the Spanish word *barbacoa*, which is in turn a variation of *babracot*, a word that comes to us from the Haitian Taino dialect of the Arawak-Carib language. The Taino word *babracot* was a noun that actually meant the framework of green sticks that formed the grill.

The Caribbean style of slow smoking on a grate over coals was brought to the Carolinas by African slaves in the 1600s and became the basis for the Southern style of barbecue. Advocates of open pit barbecue once argued that this was the only true barbecue style. Nowadays, however, German-style meat smoked in an enclosed pit, Mexican *cabrito al pastor* roasted by an open fire, and ribs grilled over direct heat all fall within somebody's definition of Texas barbecue.

All Texans agree, however, that hamburgers and hot dogs are not barbecue.

The legendary Fort Worth barbecue caterer Walter Jetton.

Today, O'Neill's Lenox Barbecue on Harrisburg Street in Houston is run by Erik Mrok, whose father was a friend of O'Neill's. The restaurant uses three rotisserie ovens of a type patented in 1967 by Herbert Oyler of Mesquite. Oyler, a barbecue restaurant owner from Mesquite, also started by tinkering with a barbecue rotisserie made from a bread-rising oven. Whether he was working independently, in competition, or in cooperation with O'Neill is not known.

Oyler's invention is a steel barbecue pit with a rotisserie inside. It has an electric carousel but no heating elements. It is fueled exclusively with wood burned in a remote firebox. The advantage of the rotisserie is that the meat gets basted with dripping fat, but it is cooked with wood smoke. It isn't exactly

Mr. White, a roadside barbecue
stand operator in Palestine, 1981.
photo by Scott Van Osdol

an old-fashioned barbecue pit, but the results still depend on time, temperature, and the talent of the pit boss. Oyler smokers are used today by well-known barbecue establishments throughout the state.

The Portable Pit

THE OIL BUSINESS, WHICH TOOK OFF IN the 1950s, had a big impact on Texas barbecue. Not only were oilmen notoriously fond of smoked meat, they were also fascinated by barbecue technology.

The backyard charcoal grill of the 1960s was fine for grilling steaks, hamburgers, and hot dogs, but it wasn't suited to Texas barbecue. In the 1970s and 1980s, a larger, enclosed style of barbecue smoker began to proliferate. It's not hard to figure out where this Texas-style portable pit came from. Some of them were just oil drums cut in half, with legs and handles welded on. Others were elaborate affairs with multiple smoke chambers, separate fireboxes, chimneys, flues, and grease drains. But all of them were made from oilfield parts.

"We made the chambers out of used oil pipe. You didn't want to know what used to be in your barbecue pit in those days," laughs Wayne Whitworth of Houston's Pitt's & Spitt's, one of the most famous makers of barbecue equipment in Texas.

"We were metal fabricators; we did big oilfield contracts. We just built barbecue pits for fun," Whitworth says. There were a lot of barbecue enthusiasts working in the East Texas oilfields. And with all that welding equipment and parts just lying around, temptation was hard to resist. "If you had all the money it has cost Brown & Root (an oilfield engineering firm) to build barbecue pits, you could feed the world," Whitworth chuckles.

Although making barbecue pits was once a hobby for the oilman, it became a successful new career. In the early 1980s, when the price of oil fell from $30 a barrel to under $10, the Texas economy went into a tailspin. "In 1983, when oil went to hell, I had my workers making barbecue pits just to keep them busy," Whitworth remembers.

"Nowadays, we can't keep up with the demand," Whitworth says. "We don't use old pipe anymore, we use new steel these days. And we can build them as big or small as you want them." Today barbecue caterers, home barbecuers, and even many barbecue restaurants use the familiar black, heavy-gauge steel pipe barbecue smokers.

Stainless Steel and Gas

TODAY, SOME TEXAS BARBECUE restaurants in large cities employ high-tech stainless-steel barbecue ovens heated by gas. A few logs are added for smoke, and the cooking process is electronically controlled. The ovens are convenient, they require no expertise to operate, and they avoid problems with air pollution regulations.

Unfortunately, no gas-fired oven has been invented that can faithfully replicate the flavor of an old-fashioned barbecue pit—yet.

Home Barbecue Rigs:
How to Choose 'Em, How to Use 'Em

COOKING TEXAS-STYLE BARBECUE AT HOME CAN BE AS simple or as complicated as you want to make it. When I graduated from the University of Texas, I had a party for my parents and friends. My roommate, the late Phil Born of Port Arthur, volunteered to make the barbecue.

Phil worked as a cook in some excellent restaurants while we were in school, so I had great confidence in him. He assembled a circle of rocks in the backyard of our rented house on King Street in Austin. Then he built a fire out of charcoal. To the charcoal, he added oak logs and burned them down until there was nothing left but smoldering embers. He stole a shelf from the refrigerator in our house and balanced it on the rocks, then he put some meat on the makeshift grill, covered it with an aluminum turkey-roasting tray, and smoked it overnight. It wasn't a very pretty barbecue pit, but the meat was outstanding.

The point is, you don't have to spend a lot of money on equipment to make great-tasting barbecue. If, however, you are in the mood to spend a lot of money, there's a really cool barbecue rig out there with your name on it.

Here are some ideas as to what's available.

WEBERS

Webers used to be great for meats that cook fairly quickly, like a pork tenderloin, sausage, or chicken pieces, but because you couldn't access the fire without lifting the grill, it was impractical to try and keep a Weber fueled for more than three or four hours.

That problem has now been solved. The newer Webers come with hinged grills, so you can lift the handle and add more wood or coals at any time. Two charcoal containers can also now be positioned to prevent the fire from spreading under the meat. This affords true indirect cooking, even with a hotter fire.

The new grill pieces run about $22 and will also fit the old Webers. A pair of charcoal containers cost about $12. New Webers are available in all styles and price ranges.

CONTACT Weber, 800-999-3237, or visit www.weberbbq.com.

WATER SMOKERS

I used to have a water smoker made by Brinkmann. It worked fairly well, considering how inexpensive it was. But smokers of this type have a few design problems. There used to be an air hole in the bottom of the fire pan, which helped the fire get air, but hot coals dropping out of the bottom of the fire pan were evidently a fire hazard. The Consumer Protection Agency made manufacturers stop putting the hole in the pan. This makes it difficult to keep the fire lit. I have seen plans on the Internet for customizing the design with a few minor metal shop alterations, but I don't know how well they work.

The problem with keeping the fire lit may be the reason that the electric water smoker has become so popular. This variety burns a little wood with an electric heating element and slow-cooks with very little effort. Not much participation on your part is required.

A new generation of gas water smokers is also beginning to arrive. The Brinkmann All-in-One is a gas grill, a charcoal grill, a water smoker with gas ignition, and an outdoor high-pressure burner for frying turkeys or boiling crawfish, all for $89.

Meco makes an excellent water smoker, and Weber makes one now, too. Water smokers are available in most hardware and department stores. CONTACT Brinkmann, 800-468-5252. Meco, 800-346-3256

BARRELS (TEXAS HIBACHIS)
Ever since the first time I went to Kreuz Market and saw those big oak logs blazing, I just kept dreaming of the day when I could start burning hardwood myself. Wood chips are fine, but I wanted a real barbecue unit—something I could throw logs into—so I bought my first barrel smoker. Also known as a Texas hibachi, a barrel smoker is a fifty-five-gallon metal drum

turned on its side and sawed in half. The steel barrels have legs and handles welded on to make them easy to use. A barrel smoker gives you enough room to burn hardwood, or at least to throw a few logs onto a charcoal fire. If you get two or three years out of a barrel smoker, you're doing fine. The tops never close evenly, the grills burn through, and sooner or later the barrel rusts out or the welds break, which is probably why they don't ship them to other parts of the country.

Some of the top cook-off competitors in the state swear that the Texas hibachi is the perfect barbecue unit. Many similar barbecue rigs are available, often made out of sheet metal but designed on the same premise—the fire is on one end and the meat is on the other. Some of them aren't very pretty, but they sure work.

CONTACT Grocery stores, hardware stores, and feed stores. Also available as a do-it-yourself kit for home welders.

BACKYARD BARBECUE PITS
For my birthday one year, my former wife bought me a big, black, heavy-gauge steel barbecue pit made by Smokemaster. The firebox and grill are on one side, and a separate smoke chamber big enough to hold a brisket, five pounds of sausage, and a couple of chickens is on the other side. The smoke chamber has a built-in thermometer on top, and there's a drain plug for cleaning on the bottom. Underneath the grill is a drawer to remove the ashes, and the chimney has a damper on it to control

the smoke flow. You can grill in it, you can smoke in it, you can burn all the logs you want. Units like mine start at around $650. This is the luxurious approach to Texas barbecue.

CONTACT Pitt's & Spitt's, 800-521-2947, or visit www.pittsand spitts.com for a catalog. Smokemaster, 512-345-7563 for a catalog. Oklahoma Joe's, 405-377-3080 for a catalog.

Houston home barbecuer Ricky Adams samples some meat from a barrel smoker in his front yard.

GAS GRILLS

Forget it. You can't smoke meat on a gas grill. I've tried those little metal boxes that are supposed to hold smoldering wood chips. I've even tried putting the chips on aluminum foil. It just does not work. If you have a gas grill and want to get some smoky flavor, get a stovetop smoker.

STOVETOP SMOKERS

An old Texas tradition is to use a discarded refrigerator as a cold smoker. You insert one of those

 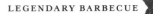

LEGENDS

Wayne Witworth
HOUSTON'S PITT'S & SPITT'S

Oil-field services contractor and barbecue cook-off competitor Wayne Witworth started out making heavy duty barbecue pits out of used oil pipe. Now he makes barcecue smokers for celebrities like George Bush Sr. and John Madden.

electric charcoal lighters through a hole drilled in the bottom on one side and stack some hardwood chips on it. Then you put some meat on the shelves, plug in the charcoal starter, and shut the door. The door seals the smoke inside, and your food gets a smoky flavor fast. Then you cook it in the oven or on a grill.

Now there's a better alternative to the old refrigerator smoker. It's called a stovetop smoker. Designed in Scandinavia, these are sealed stainless steel containers that you can use on your home cooktop. You sprinkle hardwood sawdust in the bottom, place the food on a rack, seal the container, and put it on a burner. In the tightly sealed container, the sawdust smolders without stinking up the house, and your food is smoked in minutes.

The Camerons Smoker Cooker, which comes from an outfit in Colorado, is one I've tried that works great. It comes with apple, alder, cherry, oak, hickory, maple, mesquite, and pecan "smoke dust."

The problem is, a stovetop smoker isn't big enough to smoke anything bigger than half a chicken. If you think you're going to use one to cook a brisket, forget it.

CONTACT Camerons Professional Cookware, 888-563-0227, or visit www.cameronsmoker.com.

SMOKER BAGS

A smoker bag is the single-use version of a stovetop smoker—a bag made of aluminum foil with wood dust sealed in the bottom. The smoke escapes through perforations into the cooking bag, allowing you to smoke in the oven or on a grill.

CONTACT Williams Smoker Bags, 800-255-6736.

BARBECUE TRAILERS

A barbecue trailer is a giant smoker on wheels, complete with a trailer hitch, brake lights, and Texas license plates. My daughters, Katie and Julia, have birthdays a few days apart in early April. When Katie turned four and Julia turned two, we had a huge birthday party. We

Grady Spears and
his refrigerator smoker,
Alpine, 1997.

invited over a hundred people. Of course, the two toddlers couldn't have cared less about the whole affair, except for the piñata. It was really just a good excuse to rent a barbecue trailer. For the two days that the trailer was parked in my driveway, with its giant counter-weighted steel doors and a quarter cord of aged oak stacked neatly along its edge, I was in barbecue heaven. I cooked a whole *cabrito* (baby goat), four briskets, ten pounds of venison sausage I had made myself, and a couple of pork butts. Then I smoked a big ham to have the next weekend for Easter.

You can get a barbecue trailer at many rental centers in Texas—provided your pickup has a trailer hitch. You used to see barbecue trailers at shade-tree barbecue stands by the side of the road. Nowadays, you see them mainly at catered events.

Barbecue cook-off teams build their own custom trailers and take them on the road for the summer cook-off circuit. Some of them are pretty impressive, and some are ridiculous. A barbecue trailer with a wet bar, a sound system, and a dance floor? What does this have to do with smoked meat? CONTACT Pitt's & Spitt's, 800-521-2947, or visit www.pittsandspitts.com for a catalog.

BRICK AND MASONRY PITS

Of course, a permanent outdoor smoker made of brick or cinder block is the ultimate in barbecue pits—providing it's properly designed. If you are going to have somebody build one for you, make sure they start with plans that will allow you to smoke meat. Nothing looks sillier to a Texan than a huge, expensive masonry barbecue structure with nowhere to put the meat besides the grill.

Tools You'll Need

TONGS Many cook-off competitors insist that continued forking causes meats to lose too much juice. They recommend tongs or heat-resistant gloves (see page 46). The long barbecue tongs don't handle heavy things very well. I like the short, spring-loaded kind you get at restaurant supply houses.

SPATULA Any metal one will do.

BASTING MOP Nylon brushes melt, and basting brushes are too dainty.

The best idea is to find a little cotton mop—the kind used for washing dishes.

WIRE BRUSH No, the black gunk stuck to the grill doesn't add flavor—not the good kind anyway. Clean your grill with a wire brush every time you barbecue.

POKER A stout stick from the yard will do, but you need something to move hot coals.

HEAVY-DUTY ALUMINUM FOIL

Lots of the recipes in this book call for you to wrap the meat in foil. You'll need the heavy-gauge, extra-wide variety.

DRIP PANS AND WATER PANS

A drip pan is a container placed under the meat to keep the fat from falling in the fire and flaring up. It is usually filled with water or some other liquid (such as Lone Star beer). A water pan is a pan placed in the smoke chamber between the food and the fire for the purpose of keeping a high level of moisture in the smoke chamber so the meat doesn't dry out. In a water smoker, a pan filled with water placed between the meat and the fire serves both purposes at once.

If you are cooking a meat that dries out easily, such as turkey, a water pan is a great idea. If you are cooking meat that is fatty, you may need a drip pan to keep the fire from flaring up. You don't want to use a water pan while you're trying to get something crisp.

I use a little metal cake pan, but I have accepted the fact that it will never be clean enough to bake a cake in again. Pyrex is a washable alternative.

CHARCOAL STARTER CHIMNEY

A charcoal starter chimney is a cylindrical container with a grate in the middle and a fireproof handle on the outside. (Weber makes an extra large one that suits me perfectly.) You fill the top of the container with charcoal, stuff some newspaper in the bottom, and light the paper. Within ten minutes or so, you have hot coals without using any starter fluid. Some people use paraffin in their chimney along with the newspaper, but you don't need it.

These chimneys became popular in California after the city of Los Angeles banned the use of charcoal starter fluid because it is an environmental menace. It's a culinary menace, too. If you're not careful, you end up with barbecue that smells like an oil refinery.

Note: Never put a lit chimney on a picnic table, deck, or other flammable surface.

CONTACT Weber, 800-999-3237, or visit www.weberbbq.com

THERMOMETERS As Kreuz Market has proven, if you have a big enough smoker, you can barbecue or smoke meats at very high temperatures, but a home smoker will normally be cooking between 200° and 300°F. When you are slow-smoking, keeping a constant temperature is important. My barbecue smoker has a thermometer on the smoke chamber that can be read from the outside. It's a nice feature, but you can also stick a candy thermometer through the vent of your smoker to keep track of the temperature.

When you are cooking brisket or fall-apart pork roast, the internal temperature of the meat isn't critical, but it's nice to have an instant-read, internal thermometer when you are cooking prime rib, pork loin, or other meats that you don't want to overcook.

I use an awesome cooking thermometer/timer from a company

named Polder. It uses a probe inserted into the meat that is attached by a wire to a digital read-out outside the smoker that displays the internal temperature of the meat. You can even set an alarm to go off when the meat reaches the desired doneness.

In gimmick-loving barbecue circles, even the Polder is outdone by the Remote Check from Maverick. This thermometer comes with two internal temperature probes that have heat-proof wires leading to a transmitter that sits outside the barbecue. Two internal temperatures are beamed to a handheld remote that can be taken indoors so you can monitor both pieces of meat while you watch football.

CONTACT Maverick, www.bbqgalore.com and www.comforthouse.com.

Polder, www.polderinc.com.

NEOX GLOVES Handling barbecue with heat-resistant gloves prevents you from damaging the meat with utensils and generally makes handling barbecue easier. You can find heat-resistant gloves at some barbecue specialty shops. The fabric kind get dirty fast, and barbecue competitors favor Neox gloves, which are made of washable, heat-resistant neoprene.

CONTACT Pitt's & Spitt's, 800-521-2947. www.pittsandspitts.com

Fuels

CHARCOAL The purpose of burning charcoal in a smoker is to provide a steady, long-lasting heat source. Some people prefer to start with a wood fire, which is fine, but combining wood and charcoal gives you some advantages. When you're using part charcoal and part hardwood, you can add charcoal when you want more heat or wood when you want more smoke. And since oversmoking is a frequent problem in backyard smokers, cook-off veterans like Harley Goerlitz usually recommend starting with charcoal and adding wood a little at a time. (See "Ten Tips from Harley," page 59.)

Kingsford, or any other standard brand of charcoal briquette, will work fine. Avoid the cheap composite ones, which contain paraffin or petroleum by-products. Lump hardwood charcoal is the irregular kind that's not made into briquettes. It's nice for grilling, but it burns too hot and too fast for smoking. Don't bother with the mesquite charcoal or other "flavored" varieties either. You want to use chips, chunks, or logs for smoke flavor.

WOOD In Texas, the barbecue woods are post oak, pecan, hickory, and mesquite. Pecan is a cousin of hickory. In fact, its scientific name is *Hicoria pecan*. I have pecan trees in my yard, and I have some cut-up pecan on a wood pile next to the fence. When I want barbecue wood, I take a piece of wood from the pile and chop it into chunks that will fit into my firebox. If you have hickory, maple, alder, cherry, apple, oak, pecan, walnut, or some other hardwood tree in your neighborhood, you can do the same thing, but you have to season the wood first.

"Pecan tastes really sweet, but it's sooty—it makes the meat black," cook-off competitor Tommy Wimberly told me, "especially if it's a little green."

If you are using freshly cut logs, it is a good idea to let them age a year or two. Kreuz Market in Lockhart keeps three woodpiles going. One pile is new post oak logs, another is year-old post oak logs, and the third is two-year-old post oak, which is mainly what they use for smoking.

Edgar Black Jr., down the street at Black's, mixes his woods. "We use the dry post oak for heat and some green post oak for smoke," he says. "If your meat is coming out too black, your wood is too green."

Mesquite is a completely different fuel. It is very resinous and burns hot. Grilling over mesquite is a great idea, but smoking with mesquite requires some adjustments. At Cooper's in Llano, they burn the mesquite down in a fireplace and then shovel the glowing coals into the smokers. This cuts down on the tar quite a bit. Cooper's also wraps its brisket in foil after several hours and continues cooking it on the coals. Cotten's in Robstown uses a combination of gas and mesquite, which is another way to tame the tar. If you are using mesquite for meat that takes longer than two hours to cook, you should follow their examples: Wrap your meat in aluminum foil after a few hours, or burn your mesquite wood down in a separate fireplace and just use coals. (I've heard the latter method called both "cowboy barbecue" and "fire station barbecue.")

Starting a Fire

A STARTER CHIMNEY HOLDS ABOUT TWENTY-FIVE BRI-quettes, and that's how much I usually start with. As soon as you see flames coming out of the top of the chimney, dump the charcoal into the firebox or grate of your smoker. (If you forget to dump the charcoal, the chimney will quickly burn up all your fuel, and you'll have to start over.) You can start adding wood as soon as you dump the coals. If you are using lighter fluid, be sure to wait until the coals are white before you start cooking, so you don't get any lighter fluid taste.

For a hot smoker, add about twenty-five more briquettes once you get the first batch lit. This will bring you up to about 350°F. very quickly. The bigger the pile of charcoal you light, the hotter the fire will burn.

To control the heat level, close down the dampers to reduce the heat and stablize the temperature. Then open the dampers a little at a time to increase the ventilation rate and raise the temperature.

When you add wood chunks or logs to a charcoal fire, add them to the side of the fire so that they smolder slowly, rather than on top of the charcoal, where they will burn quickly.

Direct and Indirect Heat Setups

COOKING OVER DIRECT HEAT Like open pit cooking, the cowboy barbecue style calls for putting enough space between the meat and the coals so that the meat won't burn. It's an easy way to cook a lot of meat at one time, and it doesn't take up much space. The biggest problem with cooking over direct heat is that you need a second fire so you'll have hot coals when you need to add them. (You can also use a starter chimney for this.)

To set up a grill for direct heat cooking, spread hot coals evenly across the fire box and put the meat on a grill eighteen inches or more above the coals.

COOKING OVER INDIRECT HEAT Indirect heat has become the most common style of barbecue cooking. You can set up almost any barbecue cooker for indirect cooking by putting the fire on one side of the unit and the meat on the other. A drip pan is often positioned under the meat to prevent flare-ups.

WEBERS AND SMALL SMOKERS Light the charcoal in a starter chimney. Arrange the coals on one side of the fire grate or fire pan or in the two char-

A Texas-style backyard barbecue pit burns charcoal and logs in a firebox that is separate from the smoking chamber. The temperature is controlled by adjusting the ventilation rate with a damper in the chimney.

coal pans provided. Use a drip pan filled with water. Put the meat over the water pan on the side of the grill away from the coals (or in between the two charcoal containers). Put the wood chips on top of the charcoal. Control the temperature with the top air vent over the meat and the bottom air vent under the fire, and close the other vents. Refuel as necessary.

WATER SMOKERS Light the charcoal in a starter chimney. Pour the coals into the fire pan. Fill the water pan. Put the meat over the water pan. Put the wood chips on top of the charcoal. Refuel as necessary by adding wood or briquettes through the door. Add water to the pan as needed.

In an electric or gas water smoker, put wood chips or chunks on the electric element or gas-heated lava rocks, adding a little more every few hours as necessary.

BARREL SMOKERS (TEXAS HIBACHIS) Light a fire in one end of the smoker only. You can move the meat back and forth to maintain a good cooking temperature. You can also use a barrel for cowboy-style barbecue by putting the meat directly over the fire for part of the cooking time.

When using indirect heat, the part of the meat facing the fire will be the hottest, so rotate it to keep the cooking even. Smoldering logs and charcoal are the safest fuels in a barrel. Flare-ups are a real problem. The fire can easily spread to the cooking meat and set your whole dinner on fire, so be careful about how close you set the meat to the fire. Don't overload the grill with meat. Control the fire by opening and closing the chimney damper and fuel door to raise and lower the ventilation rate. Stick an oven thermometer inside for accuracy.

TEXAS PORTABLE PITS Dump all old ashes and clean the grill surface. Drain out any old grease, and rinse the smoke chamber with a hose. Be sure ashes aren't preventing the ash drawer from closing completely and that the firebox lid and door close tightly. You need the air seal on your firebox to be as tight as possible. Excess ventilation will result in a quick-burning wood fire that will consume your fuel quickly with a minimum of smoke.

Start a charcoal fire in a starter chimney, and pour the hot coals into the firebox. Add wood chunks or logs when you're ready to cook. Bring the fire up above the cooking temperature you need, and then close the dampers to maintain a steady heat. Continue opening and closing the firebox door and the chimney damper to raise and lower the ventilation rate and the temperature. Refuel as necessary.

Cooking Temperatures

THAT OLD DOGMA DON'T HUNT
In the days of the open pit, you had to cook low and slow or your meat would catch fire, so low and slow cooking (between 200° and 250°F) became part of barbecue dogma. However, fewer and fewer pit bosses cook that way anymore.

The most famous smoker in Texas has got to be the huge double-fireplace, high-chimney pit at the old Kreuz Market location in Lockhart (now Smitty's Meat Market). In this smoker, they cook beef shoulder clods in around four hours at temperatures averaging 500°F. They barbecue prime rib in even less time. The design of smokers like this was the basis for the indirect method of cooking used in a Texas backyard barbecue rig, in which the firebox is separated from the smoke chamber. Most of the recipes in this book call for temperatures between 250° and 300°F, but some go as high as 350°F. Most backyard smokers can handle this temperature without any problem.

"You want to cook your better cuts of beef faster and at higher temperatures," says John Fullilove, the pit boss at Smitty's. "Tough cuts like brisket have to cook slow."

A barbecue pit is much like an oven. It can be set to lots of different temperatures. A brisket needs to slowly simmer in its own juices to get tender, but there's no reason to simmer a standing rib roast. It's easier to burn things at higher temperatures, so you have to be careful. But Fullilove suggests that you

pick the heat level that's right for the cut of meat you're cooking—and don't worry about the dogma.

HOW TO TELL WHEN IT'S DONE
Most barbecuers can tell when the meat is done by poking, prodding, and sniffing at it. I must confess, I have always used these inexact methods myself. While I was writing this book, it became clear that I would have to provide internal temperatures so that other people could accurately test for doneness. I decided to try the internal temperature chart that came with my meat thermometer. What a shock that was!

The recommended internal temperature for chicken on this chart is 185°F. When I tested my chicken recipes, I found that after four hours a whole chicken registered only 165°F. It looked done. It tested done by my usual leg-wiggling and knife-point insertion tests (the leg moved freely and the juices ran clear when I inserted a knife tip in the thickest part of the thigh), but it was 20 degrees short of the recommended temperature!

For the sake of the experiment, I kept cooking it. It took over five and a half hours to get it to 185°F, at which point it was black as a cinder. When I wiggled the leg, the bone came all the way out. When I carved the bird, the breast was dry. Something was clearly wrong.

I found the explanation on my cookbook shelf in Bruce Aidells' *Complete*

Meat Cookbook. Because of the scandals involving contaminated ground beef a few years ago, Aidells explains, the USDA published recommended doneness temperatures for all varieties of meat that were 10 to 15 degrees higher than those used by most restaurants.

In her cookbook *Roasting*, Barbara Kafka notes, "My temperatures are often lower than those recommended by trade associations. . . . If I cooked beef and lamb to the recommended temperatures, I would never produce rare meat again."

In this book, I provide both a lower temperature to begin testing for doneness and the higher USDA recommended temperature, for those of you who are concerned with safety.

And be warned: If you buy an internal temperature thermometer, take the doneness temperatures provided with a grain of salt!

OVERSMOKING When you first get started with real wood barbecuing, there is a tendency to oversmoke things. It's not hard to tell when meat has been oversmoked—it tastes like tar.

Resinous wood like mesquite; green, unseasoned woods; and wood that has been soaked in water can sometimes generate too much tarry smoke. If you cook with a blend of charcoal and wood or with dry, seasoned wood, you shouldn't have this problem. But be aware that there is such a thing as too much smoke.

WHEN TO USE THE OVEN

When it starts raining or it gets dark or you run out of firewood, don't despair. There is no disgrace in finishing your barbecue in the oven. Once you've gotten a nice smoky flavor and a good grill char on your meat, it will taste just as good (or sometimes better) if you finish cooking it inside. Besides, finishing your barbecue in the oven is often a good way to avoid oversmoking it.

Preheat your oven to the temperature specified in the recipe, transfer your meats, and follow the usual instructions. To hold meats that have already been cooked, wrap them in foil and put them in the oven at its lowest setting.

THE SPORT OF BARBECUE

Tips from the
Trophy Winners

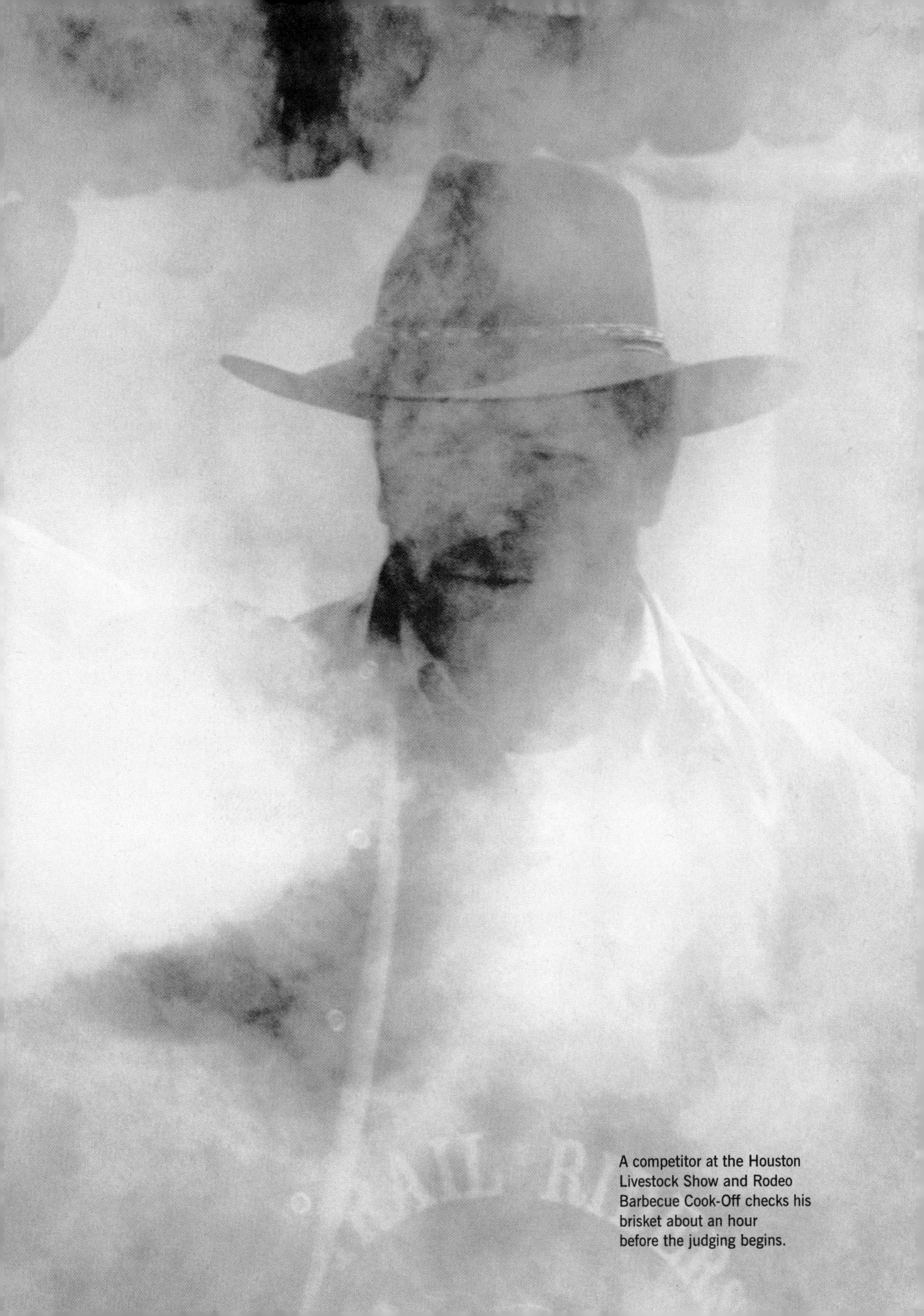

A competitor at the Houston
Livestock Show and Rodeo
Barbecue Cook-Off checks his
brisket about an hour
before the judging begins.

HE BEST BARBECUE COOK-OFFS IN
Texas resemble sporting events.
Teams from all over the state gather
to compete. And they bring with
them the cooking techniques and
philosophies of all the regions and
ethnicities that they represent.
Everybody extols the superiority of
their way of doing things, but in the
end talk is cheap—the best-tasting barbecue takes home the trophies.

There are some differences between restaurant
barbecue and cook-off barbecue. Restaurants seek to
reduce food preperation to the essentials. Few restaurants, for instance, use mop sauces anymore, because
they add to the cost of labor and food without making
a big difference in taste. Cook-off competitors, on the
other hand, take every recipe to the extreme. If mari-
nating the meat overnight or mopping it with a secret
sauce every half hour imparts one tiny iota of flavor,
they'll take that extra step.

There's a lot to learn from the pit bosses at famous
old Texas barbecue joints. Their opinions and unique
regional styles are explored in the chapters that follow.
But for the amateur point of view, it's hard to beat a
barbecue cook-off. The pit bosses of the barbecue teams
that consistently win the big cook-offs may be the best
teachers when it comes to backyard barbecue basics—

Texas pride at the Taylor International Barbecue Cook-Off.

if you can get them to talk to you, and that's generally a pretty big "if." Cook-off competitors are only interested in talking to the judges. Luckily, I happen to be one.

The 1996 Taylor International Barbecue Cook-Off was the first one I ever judged. (There were over a hundred judges, so it wasn't any big distinction.) Between my shifts at the tasting table, I wandered around Murphy Park, expecting to meet a lot of earnest competitors. What I actually found was a bunch of unshaven, bleary-eyed guys snoozing on lawn chairs beside their smokers. Good thing it wasn't a beauty contest.

It turns out that the real fun at a barbecue cook-off occurs the night before the judging. That's when the competitors stay up all night tending their fires and drinking too much beer.

For the smoke-seasoned competitors who tow their barbecue trailers across Texas each summer, barbecue is more than a cooking style; it's a way of life. In Texas alone, more than a hundred barbecue cook-offs are held each year. Winners of regional cook-offs are invited to compete in national championships such as the Kansas City Barbecue Society American Royal Invitational in Kansas City, Missouri, and the Jack Daniel's Invitational in Lynchburg, Kentucky.

Drinking beer and watching meat smoke may seem like an odd competitive sport. Of course, it is a blind tasting of the smoked meat that determines the winner. At the Taylor event, dozens of picnic tables are set up and eight judges are seated at each one. Twelve to fourteen numbered Styrofoam dishes full of

The Winningest Barbecuer in Texas

There are more than three hundred barbecue trophies in Harley Goerlitz's garage. Since 1982, Harley has won eighteen First Prizes in the Giddings Barbecue Cook-Off. He also won the coveted Overall trophy at the Kansas City Royal in 1989, the Overall at the Taylor International in 1998, First Place at the Brady Goat Cook-Off in 1991, and he was runner-up at the Houston Rodeo and Livestock Show Barbecue Cook-Off. In short, Harley knows how to cook meat. So I asked him to give some pointers to home barbecuers.

"Don't worry about buying a big fancy smoker," he said. "You can make great barbecue in a Weber, if you know what you're doing." All around him, huge, fancy rigs worth thousands of dollars were billowing smoke. But Harley was cooking in a $50 sawed-in-half oil drum.

meat are then passed around the tables and scored. The judges are not allowed to express any opinions or discuss the entries until the judging is complete.

Each contest has slightly different rules. At the Taylor International Barbecue Cook-Off, the samples get a simple 1 to 10 score. At another cook-off that I also judge, the ballot is weighted, with appearance and aroma each accounting for 5 points maximum, while taste and tenderness account for up to 20 points.

Appearance includes the quality of the smoke ring. When the meat is sliced, this band of color can be observed around the edge. The color ranges from pink to a dark red, depending on the kind of wood used and the intensity of the smoke. Judges look for both a deep color and an impressive depth.

At Texas cook-offs, the meats are sampled without condiments or sauces. I'm told that competitions in other states include barbecue sauce.

At the Taylor cook-off there are categories for pork, beef, poultry, goat, lamb, wild game, and seafood. I tasted venison, javelina, wild boar, quail, and rabbit. The wild boar tasted very much like regular pork, and the venison was excellent, but I gave my top marks to the quail.

A Texas barbecue aficionado will smoke anything. I have smoked tomatoes, chile peppers, onions, and every meat you can think of. At the Taylor cook-off a couple of years ago, I got a recipe for barbecued cabbage from one competitor. He said he had a German uncle who had been making it for years.

At first I felt sheepish asking the competitors for their recipes. Of course, some scoffed at the idea of giving out their secrets, but surprisingly, the guys with the most trophies were the ones that were most willing to tell me how it's done. As I listened to their recipes, I realized why. The secrets of prize-winning barbecue are patience, diligence, timing, the ability to judge cooking temperatures, and an instinct for what meat smells and feels like when it reaches the perfect level of doneness. Those secrets can't be stolen.

Harley's Pork Shoulder (Boston Butt)

I ASKED HARLEY TO GIVE ME A RECIPE FOR SOMEBODY who had never smoked meat before. "Tell 'em to start off with a pork shoulder. It's hard to mess up a pork shoulder," he said. Pork shoulder roast is also known as Boston butt, and it's a very common pork cut for barbecue. Here are Harley's step-by-step instructions:

1 pork shoulder roast, 4 to 5 pounds (also known as Boston butt)
6 tablespoons dry rub of your choice
2 onions, peeled
1 quart mop sauce of your choice

Season the pork roast with dry rub, pressing the spice mix into the meat, and refrigerate it overnight.

Cut the onions in half and put them in the water pan. (If your barbecue did not come with a water pan, use a fireproof steel bowl.) Add water to fill the pan.

Set up your smoker for indirect heat with a water pan. Use wood chips, chunks, or logs, and keep up a good level of smoke. Maintain a temperature between 210° and 250°F. Place the roast in the smoker.

Mop with sauce every 30 minutes, turning the roast to cook evenly. Replenish the water pan as needed. It should take 4 to 5 hours. The meat is done when it pulls easily away from the bone, but don't worry about overcooking it. It will just keep getting better. An internal temperature of around 170°F is perfect. (This is also the USDA recommended temperature.)

To serve, slice or pull the pork from the bone, removing the big chunks of fat as you go. Shred the meat by hand and serve it on sandwich rolls with your favorite barbecue sauce.

SERVES 8 TO 10

Variation: Barbecued Leg of Lamb. Substitute a 3-pound leg of lamb for the pork shoulder.

Ten Tips from Harley

You've got to baby-sit that barbecue the whole time. Stay on top of the temperature, and make sure you turn the meat often so it gets done evenly. But everybody knows all that. "What separates the good from the great is the little things," Harley says.

1. Season the meat with a good rub and then let it marinate overnight.
2. Don't use lighter fluid. Get a chimney starter.
3. Start your fire with charcoal and then add dry wood chips or chunks a little at a time.
4. Don't use a fork. Every time you poke it, the juices run out. Use tongs or a fire glove.
5. Don't oversmoke it! Too much smoke makes meat taste like a petroleum by-product.
6. Cook with indirect heat, not right over the coals.
7. If you keep the fire around 250°F, you won't burn anything.
8. Baste with a good mop sauce.
9. Put a water pan inside the smoker to keep it moist.
10. Back-time your cooking so the meat is perfectly done when you're ready to eat it. (This is always the hardest part.)

MOPS *A mop is a basting sauce. In the old days, when whole steers were barbecued, mops were essential because some cuts came out dry without them. Walter Jetton recommended that beginners use a basic basting liquid of cooking oil with a little white vinegar added. The idea was to try to replace the natural fat. Brisket, the cut of choice for many barbecuers nowadays, doesn't really require any basting, since it is barbecued with the fat cap still on it, but cook-off competitors baste it anyway for added flavor. (See Chapter 10 for several brisket mops.)*

Whole chickens can also come out dry, which is why most award-winning cook-off competitors marinate their chicken and then baste it during the cooking process. Italian dressing is the most popular dual-purpose marinade and mop for chicken. It's safest to discard the marinade liquid and use fresh Italian dressing for the mop in order to avoid bacterial contamination.

Pork cuts have plenty of fat, so pork mops don't need as much oil in them, but pork barbecuers swear by vinegar. A vinegar mop, they say, aids the tenderizing process. For a simple pork mop, you can use straight vinegar or add some crushed garlic cloves. Or you can adapt another mop recipe by adding more vinegar.

Most barbecue competitors have developed their own mop recipes that elaborate on these principles. Harley Goerlitz uses a basic mop during most of the cooking process, but adds a stick of butter to what's left of the mop toward the end to intensify the flavor just before serving.

Here is a mop sauce to get you started. You'll find others throughout this book.

Klassic Mop

THE KLASSIC KOOKERS BARBECUE TEAM OUT OF KILGORE, WAS COMPETING IN their fourteenth Houston Rodeo Cook-Off in 2001 when head cook Tommy Wimberly gave me the recipe for his mop. He keeps this mixture simmering in a five-gallon soup pot on the smoker whenever he barbecues, and he uses it on everything. You'll notice that Tommy keeps the proportions easy to handle—"I don't like measuring," he says. You can cut down the amounts to fit the size of your soup pot if you need to.

One 16-ounce box brown sugar

One 32-ounce bottle Wesson oil

1 stick (1/2 cup) butter or margarine

One 17-ounce bottle white vinegar

One 10-ounce bottle Worcestershire sauce

Large dash celery salt

1 head garlic, cloves peeled and crushed

4 to 5 onions, cut into large pieces

4 to 5 lemons, cut in half

Combine all the ingredients in a large soup pot, and add enough water to fill most of the pot. If your barbecue smoker has a firebox, set the pot on top of it and keep it simmering. If not, bring it to a simmer on the stove. Use a cotton mop to baste the meat with this mixture as it cooks. If you start to run out of liquid near the end of your barbecuing, just add a little water to what's left in the pot.

MAKES 2 GALLONS

MORE MOPS

Jetton's Beef Stock Mop. (see page 141)
Jim Goode's Barbecue Mop (see page 219)
John Northington's Mop (see page 225)

Tommy Wimberly

Veteran barbecue cook-off Tommy Wimberly of the Klassic Kookers team from Kilgore keeps his mop sauce in a pot on the lid of his firebox. Keeping the pot at a simmer prevents the raw meat from contaminating the sauce.

DRY RUBS *The simplest dry rubs are nothing but salt and pepper. The old meat markets add a touch of cayenne, too. Barbecue cook-off competitors generally favor rubs with garlic powder, ground chile peppers, and other spices added.*

Harley Goerlitz markets his own line of barbecue seasoning blends. There are also many ready-made commercial dry rubs and seasoning mixes available in grocery and gourmet stores. (See "Online and Mail Order Sources" on page 252.)

Tommy Wimberly, the head cook of the Klassic Kookers team from Kilgore, likes Tony Chachere's Original Seasoning with some Adams Malabar black pepper added. Rockney Terry of the Falls County Barbecue Team uses Adams Extract Co. barbecue rubs.

So how do you pick a rub? First you have to decide on the MSG issue. There's no doubt that MSG enhances the flavor of meat, but it gives some people a headache.

Next, check the ingredients list. For beef, you probably want plenty of salt, garlic powder, and pepper. If you're cooking chicken, you also want herbs. A pork rub, on the other hand, might have more sugar and paprika in it. You can buy a rub designed for almost any meat, but after a while you will find yourself blending your own rubs, which will certainly be a lot cheaper.

Don't use too much rub. Just as you wouldn't want to completely coat a good steak in salt and pepper, you don't want to overdo it with a barbecue rub. Sprinkle it generously over the surface of the meat. Then rub it in and allow the meat to absorb the flavor for awhile. If possible, marinate the meat in the rub overnight in the refrigerator.

Try one of these rubs for starters, then check out the other recipes in the chapters that follow.

Rockney Terry's Pork Rub

HERE'S AN EASY PORK RUB TO GET YOU STARTED on blending your own rubs.

$^1/_4$ cup salt	2 tablespoons onion powder
2 tablespoons sugar	3 tablespoons cayenne
$^1/_4$ cup paprika	2 tablespoons ground
2 tablespoons garlic powder	black pepper

Combine all the ingredients in a bowl and mix well, then pour into a shaker jar. This rub will keep for a couple of months in an airtight bottle.
MAKES ABOUT 1$^1/_4$ CUPS.

Wimberly's Real Easy Rub

HERE'S TOMMY WIMBERLY'S SUPER EASY RUB FOR chicken and beef. See "Online and Mail Order Sources" on page 252 for information on ordering the seasoning.

$^1/_2$ cup Tony Chachere's Original Seasoning
$^1/_4$ cup coarsely ground or cracked Malabar black pepper
2 tablespoons salt

Mix everything together in a shaker bottle and use as a rub on chicken and beef. This rub will keep for a couple of months in an airtight bottle.
MAKES JUST UNDER 1 CUP

MORE RUBS
Louis Charles Henley's All-Purpose Rub (see page 118)
Stubb's Hot Pork Rub (see page 121)
32 Pounds of Dry Rub (see page 142)
Rankin's Spicy Dry Rub (see page 147)
Billy Pfeffer's Dry Rub (see page 177)
Jim Goode's Beef Rub (see page 218)

Rockney Terry

Rockney Terry has been barbecueing competitively for fourteen years. He and his Fall County "Go Texan" team are always a threat at the state's biggest shoot-out, the Houston Livestock Show and Rodeo Barbecue Cook-Off. His team won the Overall Trophy at the Rodeo cook-off in 1996 and the Chicken category in 1992

Marvin Lange

Marvin Lange of Thrall is the patriarch of the Lange family and the head cook of the Smokehouse Cookers barbecue team. The family team specializes in barbecued chicken and have won more than 10 trophies in the category.

Marvin Lange's Barbecued Chicken

WISHBONE ITALIAN DRESSING IS THE FAVORITE marinade of Marvin Lange's Smokehouse Cookers barbecue team. Since they have won ten trophies for chicken at various Texas cook-offs, it's hard to argue with them. They marinate their chicken overnight and then mop it with more Wishbone dressing while it's cooking.

1 whole fryer, about 3¹/₂ pounds
¹/₄ cup dry rub of your choice
6 cups Wishbone Italian dressing

Remove the giblets and, with a sharp knife or poultry shears, cut the chicken along the backbone and flatten it open to "butterfly" it. Rinse the insides. Season the chicken inside and out with dry rub, pressing it onto the skin, and allow to sit for at least an hour. Place the chicken in a freezer bag with 3 cups of the Italian dressing and marinate in the refrigerator overnight. Remove the chicken from the refrigerator and discard the marinade.

Set up your smoker for indirect heat with a water pan. Use wood chips, chunks, or logs, and keep up a good level of smoke. Maintain a temperature between 225° and 275°F.

Spread the butterflied chicken on the grill, bone-side down. Cook with indirect heat for 3 hours, mopping every hour until done, using the remaining 3 cups of dressing as a mop sauce. When it reaches an internal temperature of 165°F, test for doneness by inserting a knife tip into the thickest part of the thigh. If the juices run clear, the chicken is done to medium. The USDA recommends cooking chicken until well done, 185°F. (See "How to Tell When It's Done," page 50.)

SERVES 2 TO 4

BRINING *Brining and curing are old meat market tricks for improving the flavor of smoked meats. What we call Canadian bacon is actually a cold-smoked brined pork loin.*

The barbecue cook-off teams that consistently win top honors always marinate or brine their chickens before cooking. Brining a chicken or a pork loin before barbecuing it is easy, and it makes a huge difference in the juiciness of the meat.

Rockney Terry's Brined Chicken

THE FALLS COUNTY BARBECUE COOK-OFF TEAM TOOK THE TROPHY FOR BEST chicken in 1992. Their secret to great barbecued chicken is brining. Brining meat saturates it with flavor and keeps it juicier during the cooking process.

8 cups hot water	1 tablespoon poultry seasoning
1/2 cup sea salt	1 can beer
2 tablespoons hot-pepper sauce	1 whole fryer, 3 to 4 pounds
1 tablespoon ground black pepper	1/4 cup Wimberly's Real Easy Rub (page 63)
	3 cups Wishbone Italian dressing

In a large bowl or crock that will fit in your refrigerator, stir the water, salt, hot-pepper sauce, pepper, and poultry seasoning together, making sure the salt is dissolved. Add the beer. Cool the mixture down in the refrigerator.

Remove the giblets and with a sharp knife or poultry shears, cut the chicken along the backbone and flatten it open to "butterfly" it. Rinse the insides. Submerge the chicken in the brine, placing a weight on top of it to keep it submerged. Keep it in the refrigerator for 24 hours to cure.

Set up your smoker for indirect heat with a water pan. Use wood chips, chunks, or logs, and keep up a good level of smoke. Maintain a temperature between 225° and 275°F.

Remove the chicken from the brine; pat dry. When the chicken is dry, rub it with dry rub. Spread the butterflied chicken on the grill, bone-side down, and cook with indirect heat for 3 hours, mopping with Italian dressing every half hour.

When it reaches an internal temperature of 165°F, test for doneness by inserting a knife tip into the thickest part of the thigh. If the juices run clear, the chicken is done to medium. The USDA recommends cooking chicken until well done, 185°F. (See "How to Tell When It's Done," page 50.)

SERVES 2 TO 4

Beer Can Chicken

A BEER CAN IS EVEN BETTER THAN ONE OF THOSE VERTICAL CHICKEN ROASTERS if you leave some beer inside—it not only conducts heat better, it also steams the chicken on the inside while it smokes on the outside. Houston's Living on the Edge barbecue team is one of the many teams that uses this popular technique to turn out moist, tender chicken.

1 whole fryer, about 3½ pounds
¼ cup dry rub of your choice
1 can Lone Star beer
3 cups Wishbone Italian dressing

Remove the giblets and rinse the cavity of the chicken. Season the chicken inside and out with dry rub, pressing it onto the skin, and allow to sit for at least an hour. Open the can and drink half of the beer. Refill the can with some of the Italian dressing. Shove the can into the chicken's cavity.

Set up your smoker for indirect heat. Use wood chips, chunks, or logs, and keep up a good level of smoke. Maintain a temperature between 225° and 275°F.

Set the chicken on the grill on the beer-can base, and cook with indirect heat for 3 hours, mopping with Italian dressing every hour. Be careful not to knock the chicken over, or the marinade will leak out.

When it reaches an internal temperature of 165°F, test for doneness by inserting a knife tip into the thickest part of the thigh. If the juices run clear, the chicken is done to medium. The USDA recommends cooking chicken until well done, 185°F. (See "How to Tell When It's Done," page 50.)

SERVES 2 TO 4

Barbecued Honey Pork Loin

A SWEETENER SUCH AS SUGAR OR HONEY IS THE MAGIC INGREDIENT IN A PORK brine. You can experiment with all sorts of sweet flavors when brining pork. Cooking a pork loin is different from cooking a pork shoulder, says Rockney Terry. Pork shoulder keeps getting better the longer it is cooked, but pork loin should be cooked just until it's done and then removed quickly from the heat before it dries out.

8 cups hot water
$1/2$ cup sea salt
$3/4$ cup Texas honey
2 tablespoons Tabasco sauce
1 tablespoon ground black pepper
1 boneless pork loin, 4 to 6 pounds
3 tablespoons dry rub for pork
3 cloves garlic, minced

In a large bowl or crock that will fit in your refrigerator, stir the water, salt, honey, Tabasco, and pepper together, making sure the salt is dissolved. Cool the mixture down in the refrigerator. Submerge the pork loin in the brine and place a weight on it to keep it submerged. Cure in the refrigerator for 36 to 48 hours. To test it, slice off a little piece and fry it. If it's overcured, it will taste salty, and if it's undercured, it won't have a lot of flavor.

Set up your smoker for indirect heat. Use wood chips, chunks, or logs, and keep up a good level of smoke. Maintain a temperature between 275° and 325°F.

Remove the pork from the brine and pat dry. Spread dry rub and minced garlic over the surface. Smoke with indirect heat for 3 hours. If you remove the pork roast from the grill at an internal temperature of 155°F, the meat will come to about 160°F after resting. The USDA recommends cooking pork to 170°F. (See "How to Tell When It's Done," page 50.)

Allow to rest for 15 minutes before carving.

Serve with German Sweet Potato Salad (variation, page 103) and Leon O'Neal's Turnip Greens (page 129). This tastes great without barbecue sauce or with Apricot Sauce for Pork (page 85.)

SERVES 10

Variations: Barbecued Maple Pork Loin. Replace the honey with 1 cup maple syrup. Barbecued Apple Cider Pork Loin. Replace the honey and $1^1/2$ cups of the water with 2 cups apple cider and $1/4$ cup brown sugar.

THE BATTLE OVER SAUCE

Disappearing Traditions
versus Modern Tastes

The interior of Louie Mueller's
Barbecue in Taylor.
photo by Wyatt McSpadden

ON'T ASK FOR barbecue sauce at Kreuz Market in Lockhart. Barbecue sauce wasn't served in the old meat markets of Central Texas, and the no-sauce tradition lives on there. Salt, pepper, and post oak smoke are the only things that touch the meat. "That's the way it's been done for over a hundred years," the current proprietor, Rick Schmidt, will tell you.

But Schmidt is not the only barbecuer with an opinion in Texas. Pit barbecue proponents always use sauce, and they don't put much stock in the methods of Central Texas meat markets. "That's not barbecueing, that's just smoking," says Chad Wootan of Cooper's in Llano, one of the state's most famous purveyors of cowboy barbecue.

Arguments over cooking methods, the right kind of wood, the correct design of a smoker, and whether or not to use barbecue sauce have raged in Texas for as long as anyone can remember. It's partly because we like to argue. And it's partly because Texas barbecue is an amalgamation of several formerly distinct styles that haven't entirely reconciled with one another.

Each of these styles of barbecue once had its own rules. In East Texas, as in most of the Old South, pork was the most common meat and open pits were favored. The woods used for smoking were oak, hickory, and its cousin pecan. In Mexican and West Texas barbecue, where goat and, later, beef were the favorites, mesquite was the wood of choice, and meats were cooked directly over the coals. German meat markets became famous for serving smoked sausages and other meats on butcher paper without sides or sauces. But the distinctions among the styles are slowly being lost.

"We started serving barbecue sauce in the early 1980s, but we only gave it to people who asked for it," says Edgar Black Jr. of Black's in Lockhart. Black's father started his meat market and barbecue in 1938, serving smoked beef and sausage rings on butcher paper with nothing on the side but crackers. But by the early 1980s, it had become too hard to explain the unusual history of meat market barbecue to all the people who were coming to Texas from other places. They wanted potato salad, they wanted beans, they wanted sauce. Black's finally gave in.

The majority of Texas barbecue joints now serve a little bit of everything. You'll always find some kind of beef offered, and usually a German-style sausage along with Southern-style pork with barbecue sauce, Mexican tortillas, West Texas beans, and sides from all over the place. Not to mention banana pudding, coconut cake, and sweet potato pie. Some places try to maintain a degree of stylistic purity, but few succeed.

That's why when you say "Texas barbecue," no one can ever be entirely sure what you are talking about. East Texas pork ribs slow-smoked over pecan? Elgin hot guts? Cowboy beef brisket cooked over mesquite? Brownsville *barbacoa*? It may sound as though we're confused, but there's another way to look at it.

The best way to preserve our traditions is to constantly disagree about what Texas barbecue really is. As long as there's some disagreement, the distinctions are kept alive.

The sauces in this chapter represent the different points of view about barbecue sauce in the state—except for the point of view that insists you should use no sauce at all.

Barbecue Joint Brisket Sauce

THE BEST BARBECUE SAUCES IN TEXAS ALL SHARE A SECRET INGREDIENT. A rare chile pepper? An exotic herb? No—the secret is meat drippings. Brisket drippings are what makes the sauce so good at Cooper's, the cowboy barbecue joint that's George W. Bush's favorite. Lots of other places I visited used the same technique.

"You collect all the juices that flow out of the meat while you're slicing and add them back to the sauce. Just like you're making a good gravy," Ray Esquivel at Ray's Roundup and QuickStop outside of Falfurrias told me as he sliced a juicy brisket.

You can't save barbecue sauce that has meat drippings in it—it goes bad quickly. The trick is to make up a big batch of basic sauce and keep it in the refrigerator. Then you heat up what you need and add the meat drippings just before serving. It's a good trick for improving bottled sauces, too.

2 cups Ancho Barbecue Sauce (opposite)
  or the sauce of your choice
Up to 1 cup meat drippings

Just before serving, heat the barbecue sauce, adding fresh meat drippings as you slice your barbecue. Do not store sauce to which meat drippings have been added.

MAKES ABOUT 3 CUPS

Ancho Barbecue Sauce

USE THIS AS A BASIC BARBECUE SAUCE, AND THEN ADD MEAT JUICES AND cut-up scraps of meat left over from carving just before serving time.

3 dried ancho chiles, stemmed and seeded
1 tablespoon olive oil
2 cups diced onion
7 cloves garlic, minced
1 cup ketchup
$1/2$ cup Worcestershire sauce
$1/3$ cup packed brown sugar
$1/4$ cup cider vinegar
$1/4$ cup lemon juice
$1^1/2$ tablespoons mustard
2 teaspoons salt, or to taste

Soak the anchos in hot water for 30 minutes or until soft. In a large, heavy saucepan, heat the oil over medium heat and add the onion and garlic. Sauté for 3 minutes, or until they begin to wilt. Add the ketchup and anchos and sauté for 4 minutes. Add all of the remaining ingredients and simmer gently for 30 to 40 minutes, stirring frequently. Remove the mixture from the heat and allow to cool. Place in a blender or food processor and purée. Serve immediately, or store in the refrigerator in a sealed container for up to 3 weeks. Reheat before serving.

MAKES ABOUT 4 CUPS

Cattlemen conversing after barbecue lunch at the San Angelo Livestock Show, 1939.
photo by Russell Lee

South Texas Ranchero Sauce

THE BARBECUE SAUCE AT COTTEN'S IN ROBSTOWN near Corpus Christi tastes like a simple tomato and onion ranchero sauce. Second-generation owner Cecil Cotten doesn't give out the recipe—but here's a ranchero barbecue sauce that has a similar taste.

4 cloves garlic, chopped
One 28-ounce can chopped tomatoes and their juice
1 onion, chopped
$1/2$ cup olive oil
1 teaspoon cayenne
Salt and ground black pepper to taste

Combine the garlic, tomatoes and their juice, and onion in a food processor. Pulse the motor on and off to coarsely grind the mixture. In a large, shallow skillet, heat the oil over medium-high heat. Pour the chopped vegetable mixture into the skillet and stir briskly for 5 minutes. Bring to a boil, and reduce the heat. Cook the mixture for about 10 minutes to reduce and thicken. Season with the cayenne and salt and pepper. Serve immediately, or store in the refrigerator in a sealed container for up to 3 weeks. Reheat before serving.

MAKES ABOUT 4 CUPS

LEGENDS

Linguistic Lore

Corpus Christi barbecue legend Joe Cotten used to tell journalists that the word "barbecue" came from the French phrase *barbe à queue*, meaning from the beard to the tail. The phrase supposedly refers to the fact that the whole animal is roasted. The reporters passed along Joe's wisdom to many readers, and this explanation is still widely circulated. The *Oxford English Dictionary* calls this particular etymology "absurd conjecture."

East Texas Hickory Sauce

BENNY WADE CLEWIS LEARNED HIS CULINARY SKILLS WHILE SERVING TIME IN the Texas prison system. Benny grew up near Palestine in East Texas. His grandfather used to sell this homemade hickory-flavored barbecue sauce in quart-sized soda bottles in downtown Dallas.

1 pound hickory chips
Juice of 1 lemon
6 stalks celery, chopped
6 heads garlic, chopped
4 baseball-sized onions,
  finely chopped
1 green pepper,
  seeded and chopped
1 cup brown sugar
$1/4$ cup white vinegar

4 quarts tomato purée
6 bay leaves
1 tablespoon salt
$1^{1}/_{4}$ cups mustard
1 cup lard or bacon drippings
4 teaspoons cayenne
1 gallon water

In a Dutch oven, combine all of the ingredients and bring to a boil. Reduce the heat and simmer uncovered, stirring until thickened, about an hour.

Set a colander over a large pot and strain the sauce to remove the hickory chips. Rinse the chips with drinking water and save the water. Use the rinse water to stretch the sauce to make 2 gallons. Reserve the hickory chips for your smoker.

Serve immediately, or store in the refrigerator in a sealed container for up to 3 weeks. Reheat before serving.

MAKES 2 GALLONS

Smolik's Easy Meat Market Sauce

BARBECUE SAUCE IS SERVED BEGRUDGINGLY BY some central Texas meat markets. I got the recipe from Bill Smolik, who grew up cooking barbecue at his dad's place, the legendary Smolik's Meat Market in Karnes City (now doing business under different ownership as Market Bar-B-Que and Fresh Meats).

3 cups ketchup
2 cups water
Dash of Worcestershire sauce
Dash of oil
1 teaspoon salt
3 tablespoons brown sugar
1 teaspoon chile powder (ground chiles)

Combine all ingredients in a medium saucepan over medium heat. Cook until the sauce begins to bubble. Serve immediately, or store in the refrigerator in a sealed container for up to 3 weeks. Reheat before serving.

MAKES ABOUT 5 CUPS

Bill Smolik

SMOLIK'S, CUERO

William Benedict Smolik is a third generation sausage-maker and barbecue man. His grandfather, a Bohemian Czech, smoked sausage on the family farm near Halletsville in the late 1800s. His father, William Harris Smolik, opened Smolik's Meat Market in Karnes City in 1918. W. B. Smolik's son, Michael, carries the tradition on in the fourth generation; he operates Smolik's in Cuero, a meat market and barbecue joint that specializes in sausage.

Pineapple Barbecue Sauce

THE SALT LICK IN DRIPPING SPRINGS IS AN OPEN PIT JOINT JUST OUTSIDE OF Austin. It was founded by the late Thurmond Roberts. His wife, Hisako Roberts, moved to Texas from Hawaii and developed a secret recipe for barbecue sauce that includes thirty-six ingredients. Pineapple juice, vinegar, and hot peppers seem to predominate. Here is a much simpler recipe for a sweet and vaguely Asian-tasting sauce inspired by Hisako's masterpiece.

2 cups pineapple juice
$1/4$ cup cider vinegar
$1/4$ cup Worcestershire sauce
$1/3$ cup soy sauce
$1/2$ teaspoon salt
$1^1/4$ cups ketchup
1 tablespoon Dijon mustard
1 cup minced onion
$1/2$ teaspoon Chinese five-spice powder
$1^1/2$ tablespoons habanero hot-pepper sauce
3 tablespoons molasses
1 lemon, sliced thin and seeded

Combine all ingredients in a saucepan and simmer until the onion and lemon are soft. Serve immediately with pork or chicken, or store in the refrigerator in a sealed container for up to 3 weeks. Reheat before serving.

MAKES ABOUT 5 CUPS

Rebekah Johnson's Grapefruit-Chipotle Sauce

I HAD THIS SOUTH TEXAS GRAPEFRUIT-CHIPOTLE SAUCE AT A BARBECUE ON A ranch near Victoria. It goes great with pork, brisket, and all kinds of barbecue.

One 7-ounce can chipotle peppers in adobo
2 tablespoons butter
1 cup minced onion
4 cloves minced garlic
1 cup Rio Red grapefruit juice
1 cup cider vinegar
$1/4$ cup molasses
$1^1/_2$ cups brown sugar
3 cups ketchup
1 tablespoon Worcestershire sauce
1 cup water
1 tablespoon salt

Remove the seeds and stems from the chipotles, and purée the peppers and their sauce in the blender. (Be careful while handling the peppers.)

In a small skillet over medium heat, melt the butter and sauté the onion for 5 minutes. Add the garlic and sauté for 5 minutes more, until the onion and garlic are softened. Add the pepper purée and all the other ingredients and simmer for 15 minutes. Serve immediately, or store in the refrigerator in a sealed container for up to 3 weeks. Reheat before serving.

MAKES ABOUT 8 CUPS

Lady Bird Johnson's Barbecue Sauce

BUTTER WAS A PRIME INGREDIENT IN OLD SOUTHERN-STYLE BARBECUE sauces. Mrs. Johnson used to send this recipe to people who wrote her at the White House.

^{1}/$_2$ stick (^{1}/$_4$ cup) butter
^{1}/$_4$ cup vinegar
^{1}/$_4$ cup ketchup
^{1}/$_4$ cup lemon juice
^{1}/$_4$ cup Worcestershire sauce
Salt and ground black pepper to taste
Tabasco sauce to taste
1 tablespoon minced garlic (optional)

Melt the butter in a saucepan, add the remaining ingredients, and bring to a boil. Serve warm.

MAKES ABOUT 1 CUP

Barbara Bush's Barbecue Sauce

BY THE GEORGE BUSH SR. ERA, MARGARINE WAS OFFERED AS AN ALTERNATIVE to butter for health-conscious barbecue fans. Barbara Bush gave out a recipe card with barbecued chicken on one side and this barbecue sauce on the other during her White House years.

2$\frac{1}{4}$ cups water
$\frac{1}{4}$ cup cider vinegar
$\frac{3}{4}$ cup sugar
1 stick ($\frac{1}{2}$ cup) butter or margarine
$\frac{1}{3}$ cup yellow mustard
2 onions, coarsely chopped
$\frac{1}{2}$ teaspoon salt
$\frac{1}{2}$ teaspoon ground black pepper
$\frac{1}{2}$ cup Worcestershire sauce
2$\frac{1}{2}$ cups ketchup
6 to 8 tablespoons lemon juice
Cayenne to taste

Combine the water, vinegar, sugar, butter, mustard, onions, salt, and pepper in a saucepan over medium-high heat. Bring the liquid to a boil and then reduce the heat to low. Simmer for 20 minutes, or until the onion is tender. Add the Worcestershire sauce, ketchup, lemon juice, and cayenne and simmer another 45 minutes. Taste for seasoning. Serve immediately, or store in the refrigerator in a sealed container for up to 3 weeks. Reheat before serving.

MAKES ABOUT 6 CUPS

Apricot Sauce for Pork

AT SUTPHEN'S UP NEAR THE PANHANDLE, THEY SERVE APRICOT PURÉE ON
the side of every meat order. You can do the same thing at home, or you can make
apricot chutney, which also goes well with barbecue. Here's an apricot-based barbecue sauce inspired by Joe Sutphen's apricot sauce.

One 10-ounce jar apricot preserves
$^1/_2$ cup cider vinegar
1 small onion, minced
1 jalapeño, stemmed, seeded, and minced
1 teaspoon salt
1 teaspoon dry mustard powder, dissolved in a little water
1 teaspoon ground ginger
1 teaspoon Chinese five-spice powder
$^1/_4$ cup soy sauce
1 teaspoon ground black pepper

Combine all ingredients in a medium saucepan and simmer over low heat
for 10 minutes, or until the onions are soft. Serve immediately, or store in the
refrigerator in a sealed container for up to 3 weeks. Reheat before serving.

MAKES ABOUT 2 CUPS

Mustard Sauce for Lamb

HARLEY GOERLITZ SAID THAT HE ONCE COMPETED IN THE LAMB DIVISION AT the American Royal Invitational in Kansas City, Missouri. Unlike Texas cook-offs, where sauce is prohibited, at this event he was supposed to submit the meat with sauce on the side. "I lost points for serving regular old red barbecue sauce," Harley said. "Barbecued lamb is supposed to be served with mustard sauce, they told me. How was I supposed to know?!"

Here's a mustard sauce for lamb, just in case you ever get into the finals.

$1/2$ cup Dijon mustard
$1/2$ cup apple juice
$2/3$ cup molasses
2 teaspoons salt
1 teaspoon crushed garlic
1 teaspoon ground black pepper

Combine all ingredients in a saucepan and stir over low heat until well combined. Serve immediately, or store in the refrigerator in a sealed container for up to 3 weeks. Reheat before serving.

MAKES ABOUT 2 CUPS

Shaker Bottle Pepper Sauce

I SPOTTED A COUPLE OF WILD PEQUÍN CHILE BUSHES OUT IN THE COUNTRY last fall and filled an empty olive oil bottle I found in the kitchen to make this traditional Texas hot sauce.

If you don't have your own pequín bush, you can substitute habaneros, serranos, or just about any other fresh hot pepper in this recipe. In Jamaica they make this sauce with Scotch bonnets and keep it in a pancake syrup dispenser.

This sauce can be used for any recipe in this book that calls for hot-pepper sauce.

$^1/_2$ cup pequin chiles (or other fresh chile peppers)
3 or 4 slices carrot (optional)
3 or 4 pieces of onion (optional)
$^1/_2$ cup white vinegar

Clean a previously used pepper shaker bottle with boiling water. (For larger peppers, such as serranos or habaneros, double the ingredients and use a pancake syrup dispenser.) Pack the bottle with chiles. Add carrot slices and onion pieces, if desired. Heat the vinegar in a small saucepan over low heat until it steams slightly. Pour the vinegar over the chiles until it reaches the top of the jar. Allow the mixture to sit for a day before using.

You can use the vinegar as a pepper sauce, or open the bottle to take out a few chiles as needed. The bottle can be refilled with vinegar about 3 times. The sauce keeps for 6 months or more.

MAKES A 12-OUNCE BOTTLE

Chipotle Ketchup

ART BLONDIN USES IMPORTED MEXICAN BÚFALO BRAND CHIPOTLE SAUCE IN his rib marinade (see Art Blondin's Chipotle-Marinated Ribs, page 181). If you can't find the Búfalo sauce in your grocery store, you can make your own chipotle ketchup. It's not only a great base for barbecue sauces, it's also remarkable on french fries, onion rings, and hamburgers.

3 dried chipotle peppers,
   or 3 canned chipotle peppers
3 dried ancho chiles
3 dried guajillo or pasilla chiles
1 small white onion, diced
5 cloves garlic, minced
2 tablespoons packed brown
   sugar, or more to taste

2 tablespoons ground cumin
1 teaspoon dried Mexican
   oregano
2 cups tomato paste
Salt and ground black pepper to taste

Remove the seeds and stems from all the chiles. Place the chiles, onion, and garlic in a large saucepan and cover with plenty of water. Bring to a boil over high heat, reduce heat, and simmer for about 15 minutes.

Remove the peppers, onion, and garlic from the pan with a slotted spoon and transfer to a food processor. Add the brown sugar, cumin, oregano, tomato paste, and a cup of the liquid the peppers were cooked in. Purée, adding more pepper liquid until you reach the desired thickness. Adjust the seasonings with salt and pepper, and add more brown sugar if desired.

Spoon the ketchup into a clean glass container and store in the refrigerator until ready for use. It keeps for several months.

MAKES ABOUT 5 CUPS

Valley Verde Sauce

THIS IS MY FAVORITE WINTER SAUCE WITH *BARBACOA* AND *LENGUA*. IN THE summer I make Pico de Gallo (page 91).

1 medium white onion, finely chopped
Juice of 3 limes
6 jalapeños, stemmed, seeded, and minced
24 small to medium tomatillos, husked, cleaned, and parboiled,
    or one 28-ounce can tomatillos
1 cup chopped cilantro
1 teaspoon salt, or to taste

In a large bowl, soak the onion in the lime juice for 20 minutes to soften the flavor. Combine the onion and lime juice with the jalapeños. In a blender or food processor, purée the tomatillos and add to the onion mixture. Stir in the cilantro. Season with salt.

MAKES 6 CUPS

Barbecued Tomato Salsa

AFTER YOU FINISH BARBECUING, HAVE YOU EVER STOOD THERE ADMIRING the leftover coals, thinking what a shame it is to waste them? Here's a sauce that lets you take advantage of those coals.

Smoking tomatoes is a great alternative to roasting them in the oven, and you can use them in all kinds of recipes. Here, they make an outstanding salsa that you can serve on *barbacoa* or *lengua* or with tortilla chips as an appetizer.

3 tomatoes, quartered
1/2 onion, sliced into rings
2 large jalapeños
1 tablespoon chipotle purée
1 tablespoon lemon juice
1/2 cup chopped cilantro
Salt to taste

Place the tomatoes, onion, and jalapeños on a hot grill, a good distance from the direct fire, and let them smoke for at least 15 minutes, turning several times. Remove as much skin as possible from the tomatoes and peppers. Halve the jalapeños and remove the seeds and stems. Transfer the tomatoes, onion, and jalapeños to a food processor. Add the chipotle purée and lemon juice and purée for 30 seconds, or just until chunky. Transfer to a bowl and add the cilantro. Season with salt. Serve immediately.

MAKES 2 TO 3 CUPS

Pico de Gallo

DOWN IN THE LOWER RIO GRANDE VALLEY, THEY USE THIS KIND OF
fresh salsa for *barbacoa* and *lengua* tacos, or for any kind of smoked meat served
on a tortilla.

5 jalapeños, stems and seeds removed, minced
1 cup diced tomato
1 cup chopped onion
2 cups coarsely chopped cilantro leaves
1 tablespoon freshly squeezed lemon juice
Salt and ground black pepper to taste

In a bowl, combine the jalapeños, tomato, onion, and cilantro. Add the lemon
juice, salt, and pepper and mix. Serve at once, or cover and hold in the refrigerator
for a couple of days.

MAKES ABOUT 2 CUPS

BUTCHER PAPER FEASTS

The Old German Meat Markets

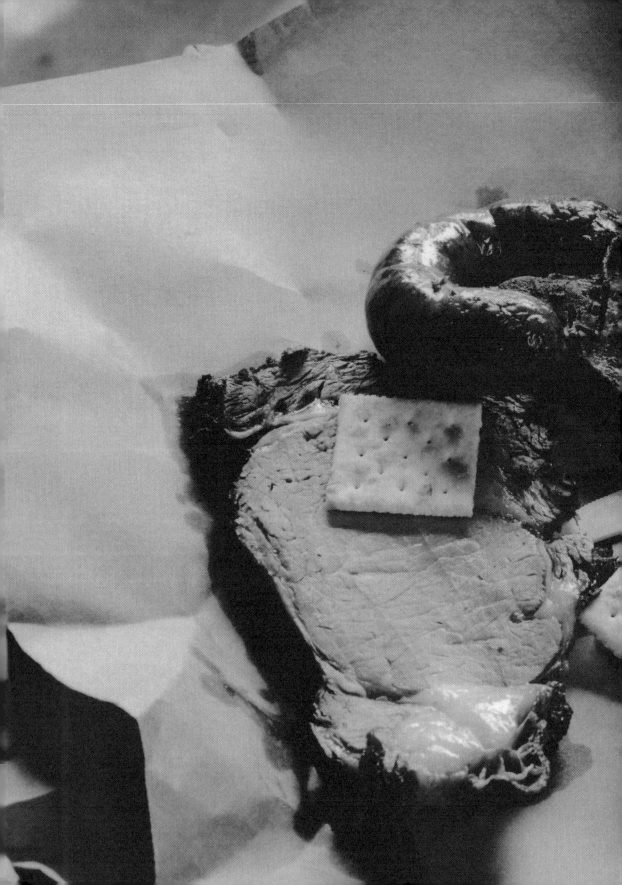

Smoked meats, sausage ring,
white bread, and crackers served
on a sheet of butcher paper
at Kreuz Market in Lockhart.
photo by Wyatt McSpadden

I F YOU FOLLOW YOUR NOSE from Taylor down to Elgin, from Elgin out to LaGrange, and south through small towns like Luling, Weimar, and Halletsville, you'll find a bunch of smoky old meat markets with German and Czech names where butchers still sell fresh chops and roasts in front and barbecue in the back. This unique style of barbecue traces its origins to the state's German and Czech settlers.

The rest of the world thinks that all Texas pioneers were cowboys. In truth, some of the fathers of the Lone Star State were political and philosophical radicals who came here from Germany and Bohemia to live on communes. The legacy of our eccentric Bohemian fore-fathers lives on in such quirky places as Luckenbach, Shiner, and South Austin.

The original Texas German pioneer was named Johann Friedrich Ernst. In 1831, Ernst got a land grant of more than 4,000 acres in present-day Austin County. The excited Ernst wrote letters to friends back home describing an earthly paradise of abundant fish and game, mild weather, and easy farming. This set off a steady stream of German immigration to Texas that lasted for the next fifty years.

Some of the German settlers were middle-class farm folk hungry for land. Others were freethinkers whose lofty ideals were suppressed by restrictive religious dogma in Germany.

These settlers, and more who followed after the Civil War, created the Texas "German belt," a large swath of German-speaking farm communities dotting the countryside from Houston to the Hill Country. By 1850, the Germans made up 5 percent of the state's population.

At the turn of the century, when the German belt was at its peak, a large area of Texas followed the patterns of Teutonic civilization. German-speaking Texans drank Bohemian-style beers like Shiner Bock and ate smoked sausage and sauerkraut.

Butchers turned their leftovers into smoked meats, just as they had done in the old country. Their regular customers took the artisanal sausage and smoked pork home and served it with the traditional German accompaniments. To a casual observer (especially a hungry one), the differences between these German smoked meats and Southern barbecue were pretty subtle.

Itinerant farm workers who came through town during the harvest bought the smoked meats at the butcher's shop and ate them on the spot. Side dishes were what they could find on the store's shelves—usually just crackers and pickles. Thus began the meat market barbecue tradition.

Some of the most famous barbecue joints in Texas, like City Market in Luling and Kreuz Market and Smitty's in Lockhart, are still butcher shops. They never did become restaurants. To this day, they offer barbecue the way the farmworkers ate it—with no plates, no knives, and no forks—just a slab of smoked meat on a piece of butcher paper.

Many other meat markets have made concessions to the popular concept of barbecue and offer utensils, plates, and side orders. A few holdouts, like Kreuz Market and Smitty's, still refuse to serve barbecue sauce. Great smoked meats don't need sauces, Kreuz proprietor Rick Schmidt will tell you. And once you've eaten Kreuz's smoked prime rib, smoked pork loin, and smoked sausage links, you tend to agree with him.

Meat market barbecue is cooked and seasoned differently from Southern barbecue, too. In East Texas, pork is often rubbed with a spice mix and served heavily sauced. Meat market pork is seasoned with nothing but salt, pepper, and smoke.

Because of its simplicity, meat market barbecue is incredibly versatile. Of course, it tastes good with barbecue sauce, potato salad, and cole slaw. But as I researched this cookbook, I wondered how it might taste the way the German-Texans used to eat it—on a pile of sauerkraut. The answer is, "Fantastic."

Here are some German- and Czech-style Texas barbecue recipes, and some eccentric side dishes like apfelkraut, red cabbage, and smoked cabbage. You won't see these in a Texas barbecue joint, but this is how German smoked meats and sausages were eaten in the old days.

J.R.MA...

CASH G...

MADE BY —
POCHYLA
and
CHOVANEC.
GRANGER
TEXAS

REPAIRED BY —
POCHYLA
AND
CHOVANEC,
GRANGER
TEXAS.

MADE BY —
POCHYLA
and
CHOVANEC,
GRANGER
TEXAS.

Butchers and clerks in front of
J.R. Machu, a Czech Grocery
Store in Granger, 1903

The old meat market at 208 S Commerce in Lockhart was known as Kreuz Market when it opened in 1900. Edgar Schmidt, aka "Smitty," started working at the meat market in 1935. In 1948, he bought the business and kept the Kreuz name. In 1984, sons Rick and Don Schmidt bought the business from their dad and expanded the barbecue operation.

Rick and Don's sister, Nina Sells, owns the building that houses the business. In 1999, Nina and Rick were unable to come to terms on a new lease, and Rick moved the business, Kreuz Market, to a new, vastly larger location. Meanwhile, Nina kept the old meat market in business under the name Smitty's.

This family feud generated widespread publicity, including a front page story in the *Austin American-Statesman* and a segment on a network news-magazine show. John Fullilove, Nina Sells's son and the new pit master at Smitty's, put the whole family feud story in a different perspective: "Kreuz Market outgrew this location," he says. "And now they have a great big new place."

Lockhart Pork Loin

KREUZ MARKET AND SMITTY'S IN LOCKHART BOTH serve smoked pork loin cooked over a hot oak fire and seasoned with nothing but salt and pepper. It's one of the best things to barbecue at home because it's so simple.

By leaving the bone in, you get a juicier roast. If you're going to use a Weber or a smaller barbecue smoker, go ahead and get a boneless pork loin roast. It will cut the cooking time down to about 2¹/₂ hours and save you some refueling.

1 center-cut bone-in pork loin roast, about 4 pounds
   (have the butcher cut the bone at 1¹/₂-inch intervals
   for easy slicing)
Salt and ground black pepper to taste

Set up your smoker for indirect heat with a water pan. Use wood chips, chunks, or logs, and keep up a good level of smoke. Maintain a temperature between 275° and 325°F.

Salt and pepper the pork roast and place it on the smoker. Allow it to smoke for 3 hours, rotating it to expose all sides to the heat. Continue cooking, checking and turning every half hour, until the pork reaches an internal temperature of around 155°F for medium. Allow the roast to rest for 15 minutes before slicing. After resting, a pork loin should reach 160°F. (The USDA recommends 170°F.)

Slice between the bones and serve the slices with barbecue sauce and fixin's Southern style, or fan the slices over a platter of Apfelkraut (page 108) or Red Cabbage (page 109), and serve with German Potato Salad (page 103).

SERVES 6

Barbecued Turkey

AT THANKSGIVING TIME, LOTS OF TEXANS TAKE THEIR TURKEYS TO THEIR favorite barbecue joints and have them smoked. Czech barbecuer Vencil Mares used to do a booming business smoking turkeys. (He's retired from the turkey-smoking business now.) This is his recipe.

"Buy a fresh turkey," Vencil advises. "Season it up with salt and pepper and garlic and put it on the smoker. I do mine for four to five hours, but it all depends on your heat. At low heat it takes a much longer time. Smoking a turkey is just like smoking a big pork roast."

You'll do best with the smallest turkey you can find.

1 small, fresh, bone-in turkey, 12 to 13 pounds
1/4 cup dry rub of your choice
3 cloves garlic, minced
1/2 onion
3 cups Wishbone Italian dressing

Rinse out the turkey and remove the giblets. Season it inside and out with dry rub and rub in well. Spread the garlic around inside the cavity.

Set up your smoker for indirect heat with a water pan. Use wood chips, chunks, or logs, and keep up a good level of smoke. Maintain a temperature between 275° and 300°F. Place the the turkey in the smoker breast-side down, as far away from the fire as possible. Put a pan full of water with half an onion in it between the fire and the turkey, and keep it full.

Turn the turkey over after 2 hours and place it breast-side up with the drumsticks pointing toward the fire. Baste it with Wishbone Italian dressing. After 2 more hours, turn the turkey around so that the drumsticks point away from the fire. Baste it with Wishbone Italian dressing, leaving some in the cavity.

Continue cooking and basting. With a meat thermometer, check the internal temperature regularly after 4 hours, and continue cooking until it reaches 160°F.

SERVES 8 TO 10

Variation: Aluminum Foil Wrap. A frequent problem with barbecued turkey is that it gets nearly black before it cooks through. It still tastes good, but it's not very attractive on the table. Kitty Crider, the food editor of the Austin American-Statesman *recommends that you cover the bird in aluminum foil while it is still an attractive dark brown and then continue cooking.*

Bryan Bracewell's Venison Sausage

EARLY HISTORIES OF THE HILL COUNTRY NOTE THAT THE GERMAN immigrants had a tough time in their first few years due to crop failures and the fact that they weren't very good with firearms. Luckily, they were great butchers, so they ended up specializing in processing wild game for others.

When deer hunters get their venison processed in the old German towns of the Texas Hill Country, some meat markets still offer to turn shoulder and other tough cuts into *rehwurst* (venison sausage) instead of the usual venison "hamburger."

You can also make this sausage at home if you have some venison in your freezer. Here's Southside Market's Bryan Bracewell's version.

5 pounds fatty pork butt
5 pounds venison shoulder, cut into pieces
$1/2$ cup kosher salt
$1/2$ cup coarsely ground black pepper
1 pint pickled jalapeño slices with their juice
Medium hog casings (available at butcher shops)

Grind the pork butt and venison together through the $1/4$-inch plate of a meat grinder (the chili plate). A little at a time, add the salt, pepper, and pickled jalapeño slices and their juice through the grinder as you go, so that they become well incorporated into the meat. In a large bowl, knead the mixture with your hands until everything is well blended.

In a small skillet, heat a little oil. Form a meatball-sized piece of the mixture into a small patty and fry it. Taste for seasonings, and adjust them as needed.

Soak the hog casings in lukewarm water. Stuff the meat mixture into the hog casings with a sausage stuffer or a pastry bag, and tie into 4- to 6-inch links. The sausage will keep for 3 to 4 days refrigerated, and up to 2 months frozen.

When you're ready to cook the sausages, set up your smoker. Sear the links over hot coals for 3 minutes on each side, or until nicely brown. Move them to indirect heat over a drip pan and smoke for 30 minutes, or until cooked through.

Serve hot with barbecue fixin's or Red Cabbage (page 109) and German Potato Salad (opposite).

MAKES 3 $1/2$ POUND

German Potato Salad

SERVE THIS TRADITIONAL SWEET-AND-SOUR potato salad warm with a garnish of crumbled bacon. Try the sweet potato variation for a very interesting change of pace.

2^1/$_2$ pounds baby red potatoes
15 thin slices smoked bacon
1 cup diced red onion
^{1}/$_2$ cup packed brown sugar
2 tablespoons cider vinegar
^{3}/$_4$ cup olive oil
Kosher salt and ground black pepper to taste

Place the potatoes in a pan and cover with water by 1^1/$_2$ inches. Bring to a boil, reduce the heat, and simmer for 20 minutes, or until the potatoes are tender when tested with a knife. While the potatoes are cooking, fry the bacon in a skillet until crisp and brown. Remove from the skillet and drain on paper towels. Pour off all but 2 tablespoons of the bacon fat from the skillet, and in it quickly sauté the onion. Remove the onion and set aside. Crumble the bacon (you should have 1 cup of bacon pieces, plus a little extra reserved for the garnish).

Combine the brown sugar and vinegar in a large salad bowl. Whisk to blend and dissolve the sugar, then slowly add the oil while continuing to whisk. Season with salt and pepper. Add the onion and bacon to the dressing. Toss the potatoes with the dressing. Let the salad sit at room temperature for 30 minutes. Garnish with the reserved crumbled bacon and serve warm.

MAKES 6 CUPS

Variation: German Sweet Potato Salad. Substitute sweet potatoes for the baby red potatoes.

LEGENDS

Bryan Bracewell
SOUTHSIDE MARKET

Byran Bracewell, a third generation barbecue man and graduate of Texas A&M, is head of sausage-making operations at the legendary South Side Market in Elgin.

Cole Slaw

KOHL IS THE GERMAN WORD FOR CABBAGE. AMERICAN COLE SLAW COMES from the German *kohlslau*. Here's a simple recipe for old-fashioned cole slaw.

6 cups shredded cabbage (about 1/2 large head)
1/4 cup white vinegar
1/2 cup mayonnaise
2 teaspoons salt
1 tablespoon sugar
1 teaspoon ground black pepper

Combine the ingredients in a mixing bowl and allow to mellow in the refrigerator for a couple of hours before serving.
MAKES 8 CUPS

Additions: Shredded carrots are a traditional addition. Shredded apples are a German addition that is particularly good with pork.

Variation: Sauerkraut Slaw. Substitute fresh sauerkraut (available in pillow packs in the deli case) for the cabbage.

Cowboys and farm workers in
the old dining room of the
Kreuz Market in Lockhart, 1979.
*Photo courtesy of Nina Sells,
Smitty's Market*

A young German butcher in
Texas in the early 1900s.

Uncle Kermit's Barbecued Cabbage

HERE'S AN OLD GERMAN RECIPE HANDED DOWN BY KERMIT SAKEWITZ, THE uncle of a barbecue cook-off competitor I met in Taylor. If you have room on the smoker while you're barbecuing something else, give this a try.

1 head green cabbage
1 stick (1/2 cup) butter
1 tablespoon salt
1 teaspoon ground black pepper
1 teaspoon garlic powder
1 teaspoon onion powder

With a sharp knife, core the cabbage, removing a good-size chunk of the tough white bottom. Rinse the cored cabbage and pull off any worn leaves. Put the stick of butter on a dinner plate and sprinkle the spices over it. Roll the butter around until all the spices stick to it. (You may need to let it soften a little.) Shove the spiced butter into the hole where the cabbage's core was removed.

Wrap the cabbage in aluminum foil so that the core end is up. Use some excess foil to form a base that will keep the cabbage standing. Place on a smoker with other items and cook for 4 to 6 hours, or until the cabbage is soft. Discard any blackened leaves before serving. Cut into quarters and serve with butter.

SERVES 4

Apfelkraut

"MY MAMA'S FAMILY WAS BOHEMIAN; MY GRANDMOTHER USED TO SERVE smoked sausage and sauerkraut all the time," Norma Moore of Cuero told me one day while she was buying sausage at Smolik's. But the Bohemians didn't eat sauerkraut straight out of the barrel (or can) the way Americans do. They cooked it with other ingredients such as apples, white wine, and bacon to give it flavor.

Here's an Old World apple kraut that's great served with smoked pork sausage or pork loin. Avoid serving this with heavily smoked meats—the smoky flavor overwhelms the kraut.

3 tablespoons vegetable oil

4 cups chopped onion

2 cloves garlic, minced

15 juniper berries

3 bay leaves

10 peppercorns

6 cups fresh sauerkraut (the kind sold refrigerated in pillow packs)

3 medium Macintosh or other sweet cooking apples, peeled, cored, and chopped into $1/2$-inch dice

2 cups apple juice

$1/4$ cup cider vinegar

3 tablespoons sugar

Heat the oil in a Dutch oven over high heat. Sauté the onions for 5 minutes, or until they begin to wilt. Add the garlic. Make a bouquet garni with the juniper berries, bay leaves, and peppercorns by tying them in a cheesecloth bag, and add it to the onion mixture. Add the sauerkraut and apples and stir well to combine. Add the apple juice, vinegar, and sugar and bring the mixture to a boil. Reduce the heat and simmer for an hour, or until the sauerkraut is very tender. Remove the cheesecloth bag, take off the cover, and increase the heat. Boil to reduce the liquid until the mixture holds together. Serve on a platter topped with smoked sausage, smoked ribs, smoked pork, or all three.

MAKES 6 CUPS

Red Cabbage

WORKING THE CABBAGE WITH YOUR HANDS IN A BRINE BEFORE COOKING will give it a beautiful deep color. The sweet-and-sour flavor of German red cabbage is an interesting alternative to barbecue sauce with a simple smoked pork loin, smoked pork chops, or sausage.

1 large head red cabbage
  (about 2 pounds)
1 tablespoon salt
2 tablespoons butter
1 large onion, chopped
2 large Granny Smith apples,
  peeled, cored, and chopped
2 tablespoons flour

1 tablespoon sugar, or to taste
1 cup red wine
1/4 cup red wine vinegar,
  or to taste
1 cup beef broth
2 bay leaves
1/4 cup strawberry jam

Quarter the cabbage, cut off the core end, and peel off any discolored leaves. Slice the cabbage very thin. Fill a bowl or nonreactive pot with warm water and dissolve the salt in it. Put the cabbage in the pot and work it with your hands until the water turns an intense purple. Allow the cabbage to marinate in the colored water for several hours or overnight.

Boil the cabbage in the water until tender but crisp. Drain and discard the water. Heat the butter in a Dutch oven over medium-high heat and sauté the onion for 5 to 7 minutes, or until soft. Add the apples and continue cooking until the apples soften. Add the cooked cabbage and sprinkle the flour and sugar over it. Toss to coat the cabbage. Add the wine, vinegar, broth, and bay leaves and simmer for 15 minutes, until the cabbage is soft and the mixture thickens. Add the strawberry jam and taste for seasonings. You will need more vinegar and sugar if you like an intense sweet-and-sour taste.

MAKES ABOUT 8 CUPS

CELEBRATING JUNETEENTH

The Legacy of East Texas

Carving barbecue to sell at a
booth at the Gonzales County
Fair, 1939.
photo by Russell Lee

AFRICAN SLAVES BROUGHT many Southern cooking traditions to Texas, including the Southern version of barbecue. After Texas entered the Union as a slave state, Southern cotton growers moved into the fertile river bottoms and blacklands of East Texas. By 1860, slaves made up 30 percent of the state's population. In some pockets, the black population was even higher—Brazoria County's population was 72 percent black in 1860.

On June 19, 1865, Union soldiers, led by Major General Gordon Granger, landed at Galveston and announced that the slaves were free. African-Texans have celebrated the anniversary of their freedom on that day ever since.

In a 1938 interview with a WPA writer, former slave Anderson Jones remembered the original freedom celebrations in which "hogs and cattle" were barbecued.

"I kin remember w'en I was jes a boy about nine years old w'en freedom cum's . . . w'en we commenced to have de nineteenth celebrations . . . an' everybody seem's like, w'ite an' black cum an' git some barbecue."

In the late 1800s, Texas African-Americans celebrated "Juneteenth," as the June nineteenth anniversary of emancipation became known, with large outdoor gatherings. These events sometimes included rodeos, prayer meetings, baseball games, and guest speakers, but they always included barbecue picnics. Barbecuing was considered a tradition that was handed down directly from the celebrations of the freed slaves.

Pork, mutton, goat, and wild game were the original barbecue meats in cotton country. Today, barbecued mutton is still seen in East Texas. But here, as in the rest of the South, pork is the reigning favorite. As with Southern barbecue, the meats are preferred falling-off-the-bone tender and more heavily sauced.

Although East Texas barbecue draws heavily on Southern barbecue tradition, it has its own distinct style.

East Texas is the only place where black Southern barbecue includes beef. Brisket in East Texas is often smothered in sauce after it is smoked and then simmered until it falls apart like pot roast. The barbecued beef sausage of East Texas, known as beef links, juicy links, or Pittsburg links (after Pittsburg, Texas, not the one in Pennsylvania), is made with finely ground beef, beef fat, and paprika. East Texas barbecue joints also tend to be proud of their side dishes, including old Southern classics like turnip greens, okra, fried green tomatoes, and others not seen in other barbecue restaurants.

Juneteenth celebrations almost died out in the early 1900s as the Fourth of July rose in importance as a civic celebration. But when Ralph Abernathy and other civil rights leaders called for an official holiday celebrating African-American Emancipation, Juneteenth made a revival. Thanks to the efforts of African-Texan legislators, on January 1, 1980, Juneteenth became a state holiday in Texas. In the last twenty years, several other states have adopted Juneteenth as a state holiday as well. As the African-Texan celebration of Juneteenth spreads across the country, its barbecue traditions will surely follow.

A slogan made famous by the legendary barbecuer C-boy Parks on a sign in front of House Park Bar-B-Que in Austin.

Harry Green

GREEN'S, HOUSTON

"My heart is in barbecue," says Harry Green, one of Houston's most famous pit bosses. "I was a barbecue man for forty-six years. I can walk into a kitchen, cut a piece of meat, and tell you how long and how fast you cooked it. I know you think I'm bullshitting you, but that's the honest truth."

Harry Green is retired now, but he once had three barbecue joints in Houston. Green's on Almeda still bears his name. "In 1953, I moved into a vacant drugstore on Dowling street (now the location of Drexler's Bar-B-Que) and built a brick barbecue pit there," he says.

Green traces his lineage as a barbecue man back through Houston's greatest barbecue artists. "I learned from Joe Burney; he had Burney's Barbecue and Avalon Barbecue in the 2700 block of Dowling. Joe Burney learned from Matt

Harry Green's Juicy Links

ACCORDING TO HARRY GREEN, BEEF LINKS AREN'T as good as they used to be; people don't like all the orange grease that flows out when you cut into them, so sausage makers are adding too little fat. Harry recommends using a combination of beef scraps and fat in a ratio of 70 percent meat to 30 percent fat.

$^1/_4$ cup salt
$^1/_4$ cup paprika
2 tablespoons ground black pepper
1 tablespoon garlic powder
$3^1/_2$ pounds beef shoulder clod or beef scraps
$1^1/_2$ pounds beef fat
Medium hog casings (available at butcher shops)

Mix together the salt, paprika, pepper, and garlic powder. Grind the beef and fat together in a meat grinder (use the fine plate), adding the spice mix a little at a time as you go. Mix the ground meat and spices in batches in a large stand mixer fitted with the paddle attachment until extremely well combined. Refrigerate the mixture.

Soak the hog casings in lukewarm water. Stuff the cold meat mixture into the hog casings with a sausage stuffer or a pastry bag, and tie into 4- to 6-inch links. The sausage will keep for 3 to 4 days refrigerated, and up to 2 months frozen.

When you're ready to cook the sausage, set up your smoker for indirect heat. Smoke the beef links at 250°F for 35 to 45 minutes, turning to cook them evenly. Serve hot.

MAKES ABOUT 5 POUNDS

Sam's Mutton Ribs

SAM'S IS ONE OF THE LAST BARBECUE JOINTS IN Texas that still serves mutton seven days a week. Wanda, Joseph, and Willie Mays are the second generation—barbecued mutton ribs is a tradition they inherited from founder Sam Mays.

They told me they smoke mutton ribs for five to six hours, but they wouldn't tell me the ingredients of their secret seasoning mix.

1½ pounds mutton ribs (or substitute meaty lamb ribs)
2 tablespoons Louis Charles Henley's All-Purpose Rub
   (page 118)

Sprinkle the ribs all over with the rub, rubbing it in well. Set up your smoker for indirect heat. Use wood chips, chunks, or logs, and keep up a good level of smoke. Maintain a temperature between 225° and 275°F.

Smoke the ribs for 5 to 6 hours, turning them often to cook them evenly. The meat is done when it pulls easily away from the bone.

SERVES 4

Garner. Matt was the oldest around here. He came from Beaumont, must have been in the 1920s. The barbecue was much better in the old days."

I asked Harry Green what was different back then.

"Nobody cooked briskets in the old days. I used to go down to the packing house and buy a front quarter of a steer. I'd cut it up myself. It was a hell of a job. And I served mutton, too. But ribs were the biggest sellers. And juicy links. Matt Garner made the first beef links around here, and he passed it on to Joe Burney, and Joe passed it on to me. It's still a big part of black people's barbecue."

"Where was Houston's greatest barbecue in the old days?"

"There were four or five great barbecue men in the old days. Matt was early on, then Joe Burney, John Davis, Tom Prevost, me, and maybe a couple of others. When the Houston papers picked the best barbecue in town, I always used to win."

Louis Charles Henley

RUTHIE'S PIT BAR-B-Q

Louis Charles Henley is the pit boss at Ruthie's Pit Bar-B-Q, a barbecue joint located in a ramshackle old house in Navasota. (Ruthie is his mom.) Louis's pork shoulder and pork ribs are justly famous in East Texas. I asked Louis for his thoughts on barbecueing.

Louis Charles Henley's All-Purpose Rub

"I USE THE SAME RUB FOR PORK, BEEF, AND MUTTON," says Louis Charles Henley. "A lot of people like to put sugar in a seasoning rub for pork. Me, I've gotten away from that. Sugar sticks to the grill, and it can give the meat a burnt taste. And in the heat of the summer it speeds up the spoiling process, too. I don't use MSG anymore either. It makes the meat tender, but too many people are allergic to it." Here's Louis's suggestion for a simple rub that you can use on everything.

$1/4$ cup Lawry's Seasoning Salt
1 tablespoon finely ground black pepper
2 teaspoons garlic powder
1 teaspoon chili powder

Combine all ingredients in a shaker bottle and sprinkle on the meat before cooking.

MAKES 6 TABLESPOONS

Ruthie's Pork Shoulder

"YOU START WITH A PORK SHOULDER, WHAT'S known in the grocery store as a Boston butt," says Louis Charles Henley, pit boss at Ruthie's Pit Bar-B-Q. "Season it up, and put it on the pit. It's done enough to eat when this bone sticks out," he said, pointing to a Y-shaped bone protruding from the meat. "But there's no big rush. I put this one on at ten o'clock last night. And what is it now, four in the afternoon?"

1 pork shoulder roast, 4 to 5 pounds
   (also known as Boston butt)
3 tablespoons Louis Charles Henley's
   All-Purpose Rub (opposite)
Sandwich fixin's:
   Sandwich rolls
   Heated barbecue sauce
   Sliced pickles
   Sliced onions

Season the pork roast with the rub, rubbing it in well.

Set up your smoker for indirect heat with a water pan. Use wood chips, chunks, or logs, and keep up a good level of smoke. Maintain a temperature between 225° and 250°F.

Smoke the roast for 4 to 5 hours, turning it every half hour or so to ensure even cooking. The meat is done when it pulls easily away from the bone, but don't worry about overcooking it. It will just keep getting better. An internal temperature of around 170°F is perfect. (This is also the USDA recommended temperature.)

Slice with an electric knife, and serve on sandwiches with your favorite barbecue sauce, pickle slices, and onions.

SERVES 4 TO 6

Louis Charles Henley on Mopping

"Oh, mopping is all right, I suppose. I used to use a mop with lots of lemons in it, and it does give a pork shoulder a nice lemony flavor. But it's not that important. And when you get real busy there just isn't time for it."

Louis Charles Henley on Wood

"Wood is the only seasoning you need. I use post oak for the heat, and then I add a little pecan for the sweetness and mesquite for the tang. Your wood has to be well seasoned, at least a year old. Green pecan will make you sick. I never use charcoal—charcoal gives people indigestion. Good wood is the only secret of good barbecue."

Monte Barber's Country-Style Ribs

MONTE BARBER IS THE PIT BOSS AT STUBB'S BARBE-cue on Red River Street in Austin. Barber gave me this recipe for country-style ribs you can make at home. He says that he can't fit a pork roast on his little smoker at home, but these ribs fit perfectly. Country-style ribs are actually pork shoulder (Boston butt) roasts cut into strips. They are very meaty, and they take a long time to cook. Don't be in a rush. To order Stubb's Bar-B-Q Sauce, see "Online and Mail Order Sources" on page 252.

2 cups orange juice
1 cup Stubb's Bar-B-Q Sauce
  (or the barbecue sauce of your choice)
3 pounds country-style ribs
3 tablespoons Stubb's Hot Pork Rub (opposite)

Combine the orange juice and barbecue sauce in a plastic freezer bag and add the meat. Allow to marinate in the refrigerator overnight. Let the meat dry, then sprinkle on some of the rub and press it into the meat.

Set up your smoker for indirect heat with a water pan. Use wood chips, chunks, or logs, and keep up a good level of smoke. Maintain a temperature between 225° and 275°F.

Place the ribs in the smoker. Turn every 30 minutes so the ribs cook evenly. Replenish the water pan as needed. It should take 4 to 5 hours. The meat is done when it pulls easily away from the bone, but don't worry about overcooking it. It will just keep getting better. An internal temperature of around 170°F is perfect. (This is also the USDA recommended temperature.)

SERVES 4 TO 6

Stubb's Hot Pork Rub

STUBB HAS PASSED AWAY, BUT STUBB'S BARBECUE on Red River street in Austin tries to keep his spirit alive. This is the restaurant's recipe for hot pork rub.

1 cup salt
$1/4$ cup chili powder
$1/4$ cup paprika
$1/3$ cup garlic powder
$1/3$ cup cayenne
$1/2$ cup ground dry rosemary
$1/2$ cup ground black pepper

Combine all ingredients and store in a shaker.
MAKES ABOUT 2²/₃ CUPS

Louis Charles Henley on Parboiling

"In the old days, a lot of folks in East Texas parboiled pork before they barbecued it. Parboiling speeds up the cooking and makes the meat really tender, but it takes a lot of the flavor away. Of course, you have to remember that sometimes folks in the old days were barbecuing a bull hog. You've got to parboil something with that much scent to it. There are still plenty of barbecue places that parboil their ribs. They just won't admit it."

Louis Charles Henley on Aluminum Foil

"In a brick pit, you don't have to worry about burning things. But when I run a steel pit, I cook at 350 degrees until the outside of the meat looks good, and then I wrap it up in foil. The foil will make the meat split open and get too tender, but at least you don't burn it."

Passing the time in front of
New Zion Missionary Church
Barbecue in Huntsville.

House Park Pork Loin Sandwiches

THE TINY BARBECUE JOINT IS NAMED AFTER THE HIGH SCHOOL FOOTBALL
stadium next door. A House Park Pork Loin Sandwich on the picnic tables out
front near 12th Street is an Austin tradition. For a new twist, try a pork loin
sandwich on Fried Green Tomatoes (oppposite).

1 pound Lockhart Pork Loin, sliced (page 100)
1 cup barbecue sauce of your choice
4 hamburger rolls
Salt and ground black pepper to taste
$1/2$ sweet onion, thinly sliced
8 pickle slices

Remove the roast from the heat and allow to stand 15 minutes before carving.
Heat the barbecue sauce. Cut the loin across the grain into thin slices on a carving
board with a well, collecting the drippings as you go and adding them to the
heated sauce. Dip each half of the hamburger bun into the barbecue sauce. Layer
the loin slices onto the bottom bun, sprinkling with salt and pepper as you pile.
Top with onion and pickle slices.

MAKES 4 SANDWICHES

Fried Green Tomatoes

SOME FOLKS LIKE TO MAKE THEIR PORK LOIN SANDWICHES OUT OF FRIED green tomatoes. You put a layer of pork and barbecue sauce between two fried green tomato slices. Pick it up if you want, or eat it with a fork and knife.

2 cups peanut oil
1 cup finely ground cornmeal
Salt and ground white pepper to taste
2 eggs, beaten with 2 tablespoons of water
4 green tomatoes, thickly sliced

In a heavy-bottomed pot, heat the peanut oil to 350°F. Place the cornmeal on a plate and season with salt and white pepper. Place the beaten egg mixture in a shallow dish, such as a pie plate. Drop the green tomato slices in the egg mixture and then pat them in the cornmeal to coat. Place the tomato slices in the hot oil in batches and fry for 2 to 3 minutes, turning over once during the frying. Remove the slices from the fryer and allow to cool slightly on a wire mesh rack. Serve immediately.

MAKES ABOUT 12 TOMATO SLICES

Mashed Potato Salad

POTATO SALAD IS SOFT AND FLUFFY IN EAST TEXAS. THEY SERVE IT WITH AN ice cream scoop at New Zion Missionary Baptist Church Barbecue. It tastes best when it's still warm.

1 1/2 pounds russet potatoes
1/2 cup mayonnaise
2 green onions, sliced
1 tablespoon pickle relish
4 teaspoons pickle juice
4 teaspoons hot-pepper sauce
Salt to taste

Peel the potatoes and cut them into 1-inch chunks. Place the potatoes and enough water to cover in a 4-quart saucepan. Bring to a boil over high heat. Cover and simmer 15 minutes, or until the potatoes are tender. Drain.

In a large bowl, coarsely mash the potatoes. Stir in the remaining ingredients. Serve at room temperature.

SERVES 4

Wanda Mays and friends in front of Sam's BBQ in Austin.

Huntsville Butter Beans

YOU'LL FIND PINTO BEANS SERVED WITH BARBECUE ALL OVER THE STATE, but New Zion Missionary Baptist Church Barbecue is the only place I've had Southern-style lima beans.

1 pound dried lima beans
1 onion, diced
1 ham hock (or 6 slices bacon, diced)
Salt and ground black pepper to taste

Sort the beans and rinse them well. Soak them overnight in water and discard the water. Combine the soaked beans with the onion and ham hock and cover with water in a crockpot or slow cooker. Cook on high for 1 hour, and then turn the heat to low and simmer for 4 to 5 hours, or until meltingly tender. Season with salt and pepper.

SERVES 6

Leon O'Neal's Turnip Greens

AT LEON'S "WORLD'S FINEST" IN & OUT B-B-Q HOUSE ON GALVESTON ISLAND, they serve tender ribs and tangy sauce with sensational Southern-style vegetables. "It's all in the seasoning," says Leon. Here's his recipe for turnip greens.

1 large bunch turnip greens
1 small turnip, peeled and diced
Dash of sugar
6 slices bacon, diced
1 onion, diced
1 tablespoon lemon pepper
Salt to taste
Louisiana hot-pepper sauce

Wash the greens in several changes of water in the sink until no more grit is seen. Chop the greens coarsely. Bring a large pot of water to a boil and add the greens, the turnip, and the sugar. Cook for 12 to 15 minutes, or until tender. Drain.

In a large skillet, sauté the bacon until it gives up its grease. Add the onion and cook 7 minutes until the onion is soft. Toss the greens with the bacon and onion. Add the lemon pepper and salt. Serve with Louisiana hot-pepper sauce.

SERVES 4

Variation: Green Beans. Substitute 1 pound fresh green beans, cleaned and snapped. Omit the sugar.

Leon's Stepped-Up Rice

IF YOU WANT SOMETHING DIFFERENT FROM THE USUAL BEANS OR POTATO salad, try this tasty rice dish, which Leon offers at his In & Out B-B-Q House.

3 jalapeños, seeded and coarsely chopped
1 onion, coarsely chopped
3 ribs celery, chopped
1 bell pepper, seeded and chopped
2 tablespoons peanut oil
4 cups freshly cooked Texmati rice

Combine the jalapeños, onion, celery, and bell pepper in a food processor and pulse several times to make a finely chopped vegetable paste.

Heat the oil in a large skillet and fry the paste for 5 to 7 minutes, or until soft. Add the hot rice and blend well.

MAKES ABOUT 5 CUPS

Senator Lloyd Bentsen Highway Rice Salad

BARBECUE JOINTS IN THE RICE-GROWING REGION ALONG HIGHWAY 59 (Senator Lloyd Bentsen Highway) between Houston and Victoria all serve some kind of rice salad along with the usual potato and macaroni salads. Here's a modern version.

3 cups freshly cooked Texmati rice

$1/2$ cup vinaigrette (or Italian dressing)

$1/2$ cup chopped tomato

$1/2$ cup chopped celery

$1/2$ cup chopped green pepper

$1/4$ cup diced carrot

$1/4$ cup chopped red onion

1 cup peeled, seeded, and chopped cucumber

$1/2$ cup chopped black olives

1 tablespoon hot-pepper sauce

1 teaspoon mustard

$1/2$ cup plain yogurt

$1/2$ cup chopped toasted pecans

3 tablespoons chopped cilantro

Toss the hot rice with the vinaigrette and refrigerate. When it's cool, combine with the remaining ingredients, except the pecans and cilantro, and mix well. Serve garnished with the pecans and cilantro.

SERVES 8

THE LAST OF
THE OPEN PITS

West Texas Cowboy Barbecue

Cattlemen at a barbecue held at the Pitchfork Land and Cattle Company near Guthrie in 1976.

HE CATTLE INDUSTRY GOT its start in 1867 when cowboys took their first herd up the Chisholm Trail to Kansas. Within a few years, millions of longhorns had been rounded up and taken to market. After the Comanches and the buffalo were killed off, cattlemen took over the vast grasslands of western Texas. Enormous ranches of hundreds of thousands of acres were tended by just a handful of cowboys.

Barbecuing whole steers was already popular at civic barbecues before the Civil War. After the war, thanks to the emerging Texas cattle industry, the market was flooded with beef. In 1873, the best beef cuts were selling for four cents a pound at meat markets in Austin. The lesser cuts were what people used for barbecue.

The steer's forequarters were typically cut into six- to eight-pound joints and cooked over hot coals in an open pit, but the lean range-fed beef required continuous basting for up to twenty-four hours. A cotton mop was used, and the basting liquid, generally cooking oil and a little vinegar, was mixed in buckets.

Long after urban barbecue restaurants began to move their cooking into enclosed pits for sanitary

Eating barbecue during round-up
at Sheriff Travis Hogue Pool's
Ranch in La Salle County, 1941.

Cowboy-style ribs are cooked directly over hot coals at a barbecue at the LBJ Ranch.

reasons, West Texans continued to cook outdoors. Chuck wagon cooks simmered beans and other long-cooking foods in cast iron Dutch ovens. Meat was barbecued on a grate over an open pit in the old-fashioned style. While cooking in trenches was outlawed for restaurants, it remained common for large catered barbecue events until the 1960s.

Walter Jetton, the most famous of the cowboy-style barbecuers, came to the attention of the American public after catering a dinner for the president-elect of Mexico held by Lyndon Johnson. In magazine articles and cookbooks, Jetton baffled Americans by insisting that if they wanted to make real Texas barbecue, they had to dig holes in their backyards. In one magazine interview, Jetton told would-be barbecue enthusiasts, "To barbecue, you need a pit. . . and it definitely shouldn't be one of those backyard creations with a chimney."

Jetton was also a proponent of slow cooking in open pits. In this style of barbecue, "low and slow" was indeed the only way to go. By using coals instead of flaming wood, you avoided flare-ups that would burn the meat. In the days when whole steers or fore-quarters were cut up for barbecuing, long, slow cooking guaranteed that even the toughest cuts got tender.

Eventually Jetton, like most Texas barbecuers, abandoned whole steer barbecue in favor of brisket. From Walter Jetton's point of view, brisket was practically a convenience food. In a letter to Larry Hunt, a lumberman in Minnesota who was looking for advice on barbecuing half steers, Jetton wrote, "First we would suggest you abandon the idea of a spit and instead of trying to barbecue the beef in quarters or halves, just buy eight- to ten-pound pieces of bone-less brisket points." The fat layer attached to a brisket melts slowly as the meat cooks. Jetton called brisket a "self-basting cut."

Jetton's state dinner at the Pedernales White House may be the most prestigous barbecue of all time.

America's First State Barbecue

Menu for the barbecue given by President and Mrs. Lyndon B. Johnson honoring the President-elect of Mexico and Mrs. Gustavo Diaz Ordaz, held on the banks of the Pedernales River at the LBJ Ranch at 1 P.M., Thursday, November 12, 1964.

Barbecued brisket
Barbecued pork ribs
Barbecued chicken
Hot link sausage
Ranch-style beans
Sourdough biscuits
German potato salad
Texas cole slaw
Dill pickles
Sliced onions
Fried apple pie
Iced tea
Six-shooter coffee

Walter Jetton's
Barbecued Beef for 250

WHILE A BARBECUE FOR A COUPLE OF HUNDRED PEOPLE WAS NO BIG DEAL IN Texas, the rest of the country was fascinated by the doings down at the LBJ Ranch. Magazines and newspapers featured Texas barbecue recipes, and the White House received letters asking for tips. Here's a recipe derived from Walter Jetton's advice.

35 top-quality beef briskets, about
    10 pounds each, or 300 pounds
    beef, cut into 6- to 8-pound pieces
10 pounds dry rub, or to taste
6 gallons Jetton's Beef Stock Mop
  (opposite)
Heated barbecue sauce

Sandwich fixin's:
  Sandwich rolls
  Sliced pickles
  Sliced pickles
  Sliced onions

Dig a pit 3-feet-deep, 4-feet-wide, and 40-feet-long. Place a layer of wood (any type of hardwood can be used) across the bottom of the pit, and start the fire. Keep the fire at the same height for about 5 hours and then let it die down to coals.

Place iron pipe across the pit every 3 feet and cover with heavy wire mesh. Make sure that the mesh is securely tied so that the meat won't get dumped into the fire. Make a 1-foot opening under the wire at intervals, through which additional coals can be added. Start another fire to one side so that additional coals will be available.

Season generously with the rub, and rub in well. Place the meat on the wire mesh. Do not overlap; leave plenty of room for smoke to come up. Baste with the mop sauce every half hour. Throw a little water on the coals once or twice during the cooking process to steam the meat with intense, moist heat.

Turn the meat frequently so that it will cook evenly, and allow at least 18 hours' cooking time. Do not allow any blaze after the meat is put on—only coals!

Allow the meat to rest 15 minutes before carving. Slice it thinly against the grain and serve with barbecue sauce and sandwich fixin's.

Jetton's Beef Stock Mop

JETTON STARTED HIS MOP SAUCE WITH A BEEF STOCK MADE FROM THE BONES left over from the butchering of the steer. He used a full-sized cotton mop to baste hundreds of pounds of meat; for home cooks, however, he recommended miniature cotton mops used for dishwashing. Those little cotton mops aren't used much for dishes anymore, but you can still find them in barbecue and kitchen-goods stores.

4 gallons beef stock
$3/4$ cup salt
$3/4$ cup dry mustard powder
$1/2$ cup garlic powder
$1/4$ cup ground bay leaf
$1/2$ cup chili powder
$3/4$ cup paprika
$1/2$ cup hot-pepper sauce
2 quarts Worcestershire sauce
2 quarts vinegar
2 quarts oil
$3/4$ cup MSG

Combine all ingredients and let stand overnight before using to baste barbecued meats.

MAKES ABOUT 8 GALLONS

32 Pounds of Dry Rub

SALT COMES IN 25-POUND BAGS, SO MOST OF THE barbecue rubs in the old days started with this quantity. Here's an old meat market recipe for dry rub.

25 pounds salt
1 pound chili powder
2 pounds sugar

3 pounds coarsely
    ground black pepper
1 pound garlic powder

Combine all ingredients and store in an airtight container. Rub on meats before barbecuing.

MAKES 32 POUNDS

Texas-Size Cole Slaw

HERE'S A LARGE-QUANTITY RECIPE FOR OLD-fashioned cole slaw. It gets better as it sits.

12 heads green cabbage
6 pounds carrots
1/4 cup salt
2 cups sugar
1 tablespoon garlic powder

2 tablespoons ground black
    pepper
2 cups white vinegar
8 cups mayonnaise

Shred the cabbage and carrots and combine in a plastic food storage barrel (or several smaller containers) with the other ingredients. Allow to mellow in the refrigerator for a few hours before serving, mixing every half hour.

MAKES ABOUT 20 POUNDS

A Cowboy Barbecue

"Nine months of the year . . . you didn't see hide nor hair of the headquarters. You saw the ram rod . . . you saw the foreman . . . but what you didn't see was any signs of civilization. I put in five years with about the same routine.

"We boys began hearing rumors that the railroad was going to have a big dance and barbecue when the end of the line reached O'Donnell (in 1912). Well, that was all I wanted to know. A dance and a barbecue! At the end of the day there was at least 5,000 people there. Tons of meat was barbecued in advance, but not near enough."

—FRANK MARCH, WPA INTERVIEW, 1938

Walter Jetton serves up a plate to LBJ and guests at America's first barbecue state dinner.

Lorenzo Vences

**COOPER'S OLD TIME
PIT BAR-B-Q**

"Mesquite coals give the meat a lot of flavor without over smoking it." says Lorenzo Vences, pit boss at Cooper's in Llano since 1986. "This is the best barbecue in Texas."

Lorenzo Vences' Sirloin

COOPER'S OLD TIME PIT BAR-B-Q IN LLANO HAS preserved the "cowboy barbecue" open pit–style. At Cooper's, mesquite wood is burned down to coals in a fireplace and the coals are shoveled into enclosed pits. The meat is cooked by direct heat about 28 to 30 inches above the coals with the lid closed. When the steak is done to 140°F, it is moved to a holding pit where it continues to cook slowly until it is sold. Pit boss Lorenzo Vences estimates the heat in his pit at 350° to 400°F.

Cowboy barbecue is a cross between grilling and smoking. You start the meat over the coals and move it when the color is right—then finish cooking it with indirect heat.

1 USDA Choice beef sirloin steak,
  2 to 2½ pounds and 1¾ inches thick,
  (branded beef such as Black Angus or
  Certified Hereford preferred)
or
1 USDA Choice beef sirloin tip roast,
  2 to 2½ pounds (branded beef such as Black Angus or
  Certified Hereford preferred)
Salt and coarsely ground black pepper to taste

Allow the meat to come to room temperature and season it with salt and pepper. Light mesquite chunks in a starter chimney. Pour the hot coals into your firebox. Light another batch of mesquite chunks a few minutes later. Maintain a temperature between 350° and 400°F, and place the meat at least 18 inches above the coals until it's well browned, or until it reaches an internal temperature of 120°F. Add more coals as needed. Douse flare-ups with a squirt bottle.

When the steak is well charred, move it to a cooler part of the barbecue where it can cook indirectly until it reaches the desired temperature. Remove it from the smoker when it is firm to the touch, between 135° and 140°F. The meat will continue to cook after it is removed, so allow it to rest before carving. At 140°F, the meat will be medium-rare. Cooper's won't serve any meat that hasn't reached 140°F. (This is the USDA recommended temperature for rare.) Remove the meat at 145°F for medium and 155°F for medium-well.

SERVES 4 TO 6

Variation: Cooper's "Big Chop" Cowboy Pork Chops. Substitute 2-inch-thick double-cut bone-in pork loin chops for the sirloin. Move them to a cooler spot when they reach 145°F, and remove them from the grill at 155°F.

Spanish shepherds raised cattle for money, sheep for wool, and goats for meat. The herders brought this tradition along with livestock to Texas and Northern Mexico in the late 1600s. In 1765, a Spanish census counted tens of thousands of head of cattle, sheep, and goats belonging to the Spanish missions on the South Texas plains.

The Spanish *pastores*, or shepherds, adapted their style of herding to the vast distances by working on horseback. The mounted shepherds became known as *vaqueros*, which we translate as "cowboys."

After the missions were abandoned, the livestock proliferated in the wild. At the end of the Civil War, there were some three million longhorns in Texas. The early Texas cowboys who went to herd these wild cattle adopted the clothing, saddlery, and roping techniques of the vaqueros. They were called "buckaroos," a mispronunciation of "vaqueros."

A few cowboys out "cow hunting" couldn't eat a whole longhorn, so they followed the example of the vaqueros and ate goat. An eighteen- or twenty-pound *cabrito* is just the right amount of meat for a few cowboys at dinner time, which is why goat meat has remained a favorite of cowboys to this day.

Barbecued Goat

THE BRADY GOAT COOK-OFF IS A BARBECUE contest devoted exclusively to goat. It's held every year over Labor Day weekend. Lonnie Rankin of Miles, won this contest for the first time in 1983. Since then, he and his team, Miles Messenger Messy Cookers, have won the annual Brady Superbowl (open only to previous winners) in 1991 and again in 1999. This is Lonnie's simplified recipe, for people who want to try to barbecue goat in the backyard.

Goat hindquarter cut into 1-inch steaks (2$^1/_2$ to 3 pounds)
$^1/_4$ cup Rankin's Spicy Dry Rub (opposite)
2 sticks (1 cup) butter, melted

Rub the goat steaks with the dry rub and allow them to come to room temperature. Light your barbecue. Use wood chips, chunks, or logs, and keep up a good level of smoke. Maintain a temperature between 275° and 325°F.

Start the steaks directly over the fire until you get a nice color, then move them to indirect heat. Turn and brush the steaks with butter every 30 to 45 minutes. If the fire gets hot, turn them quicker. Keep tasting the meat—it should get tender after 3 or 4 hours. If the USDA has a recommended temperature for a goat, I've never heard about it. I'd start testing it at around 155°F, but be aware that there's not much fat in a goat, so if you cook it too long, it will dry out. Great barbecued goat is all a matter of timing.

SERVES 4 TO 6

Rankin's Spicy Dry Rub

YOU PROBABLY DON'T LIKE MSG IN YOUR FOOD, BUT YOU PROBABLY DON'T cook much goat either. Substitute a meat tenderizer that doesn't contain MSG if you prefer.

$1/2$ cup salt

$1/3$ cup ground black pepper

$1/4$ cup paprika

$1/4$ cup chili powder

$1/2$ cup garlic powder

2 tablespoons MSG

Combine all ingredients in a shaker bottle. This mixture will keep for a couple of months.

MAKES ABOUT 2 CUPS

Lonnie Rankin's Ranch Potatoes

"AT HOME WE EAT BARBECUED GOAT WITH SPICY BEANS, RANCH POTATOES, and our own homemade barbecue sauce," says Lonnie Rankin. Here's his recipe for potatoes.

3 russet potatoes,
    sliced $1/2$ inch thick

1 tablespoon olive oil

1 tablespoon chili powder

1 teaspoon salt

1 teaspoon ground black pepper

Preheat the oven to 350°F. Put the potato slices in a baking pan and drizzle the oil over them. Combine the chili powder, salt, and pepper, and sprinkle on the potatoes. Shake the pan to coat the potatoes all over. Bake, turning with a spatula every 10 minutes, until crispy, about 40 minutes.

SERVES 4

Jalapeño Potato Salad

BEVERLY BUNDY IS THE FOOD EDITOR OF THE *FORT Worth Star-Telegram*. Here's her recipe for a spicy West Texas potato salad.

4 large potatoes, peeled and cut into ³/₄-inch cubes
¹/₄ cup Dijon mustard
¹/₄ cup white wine vinegar
2 cloves garlic, crushed
¹/₄ teaspoon salt
¹/₄ teaspoon ground black pepper
¹/₂ cup olive oil
One 3¹/₂-ounce can pitted black olives, drained
¹/₄ cup thinly sliced scallions
6 ounces feta cheese, crumbled
4 jalapeños, seeded and chopped

Place the potatoes in a 3-quart saucepan or Dutch oven and pour in cold water to cover. Bring to a boil. Reduce the heat to low and simmer for 10 minutes, or until the potatoes are tender. Drain.

Meanwhile, in a large bowl, combine the mustard, vinegar, garlic, salt, and pepper. Slowly whisk in the oil. Add the potatoes, olives, scallions, feta cheese, and jalapeños. Toss to mix well.

Serve chilled or at room temperature.

SERVES 6

LEGENDS

Mayonnaise Myths

Forget the urban myth about the mess sergeant who poisoned his entire platoon by serving them potato salad that had been on maneuvers all day. Commercial mayonnaise uses pasteurized eggs and contains acids (vinegar, lemon, and salt) that actually kill bacteria that grow in food. Homemade mayonnaise is another scenario, but it would be heresy to use it in potato salad.

The cook is a more likely the culprit in mass outbreaks of food poisoning. Adding cold mayonnaise to hot potatoes sets up a prime breeding ground for bacteria, which flourish at 40° to 145°F. Instead, refrigerate potato salad as soon as it's prepared, to quickly cool it down. For best flavor, remove it from the refrigerator and allow it to come to room temperature before serving.
—BEVERLY BUNDY

Mustard Potato Salad

YOUR CHOICE OF MUSTARD MAKES A BIG DIFFERENCE IN THIS RECIPE. THEY like yellow potato salad in West Texas, so they use a bright yellow mustard like French's. German coarse-ground mustard gives the potato salad a darker color and a heartier flavor. French Dijon mustard makes it pretty hot.

8 russet potatoes
8 hard-boiled eggs, chopped
1 cup chopped onion
1 cup chopped celery
3 tablespoons chopped parsley
2 teaspoons celery seed
3 tablespoons mustard
2^1/$_2$ cups mayonnaise
Salt and ground black pepper to taste

Place the unpeeled potatoes in a large pot and pour in cold water to cover. Bring to a boil. Reduce the heat to low and simmer for 20 minutes, or until the potatoes are tender. Drain.

Peel the potatoes while still slightly hot, and cut into chunks. Place in a large bowl and add the chopped eggs, onion, celery, parsley, celery seed, mustard, and mayonnaise, plus salt and pepper.

Serve chilled or at room temperature.

SERVES 12

FEEDING THE COTTON PICKERS

The Rise of the Barbecue Business

Cotton pickers on their way home to Mexico stop for a snack and a cold drink at a filling station.
Photo by Russell Lee

COTTON PICKERS TURNED Texas barbecue into a big business. From the the late 1800s until cotton picking was mechanized in the early 1960s, migrant workers picked their way across the Texas cotton belt every year, beginning in the Lower Rio Grande Valley, where cotton ripened in late June, and working their way up to Lubbock, where the cotton was ready to harvest in September.

In 1938, the number of migrant workers in the state was estimated at around six hundred thousand. The monumental task of feeding this army gave rise to the first generation of Texas barbecue entrepeneurs.

The pickers descended on the grocery stores and meat markets of the small towns where they worked, looking for anything that was ready to eat. Their favorites were the smoked cuts and sausages at the meat market, which they ate right off of the butcher paper with crackers, white bread, pickles, and whatever else they could find on the store's shelves.

"My daddy, William Harris Smolik, opened Smolik's Meat Market in Karnes City in 1918," remembers William Benedict (Bill) Smolik. "The pickers ate barbecue at our place for breakfast, lunch,

Cotton pickers in a field near San Antonio, 1930.

LEGENDS

The Long Walk

"Mexican cotton pickers . . .
picked the cotton in the Lower
Rio Grande Valley and then
moved northward, picking cotton as it matured and eventually winding up in East
Texas . . . When the cotton was
all picked, they would walk
back . . . to Mexico."
—J.K.WELLS
in an interview with John and
Ruby Lomax, 1939

and dinner in those days. Dad used to keep the money in a bushel basket during cotton picking season, and it was my job to count it. I remember one Saturday we made a thousand dollars in one day, selling barbecue at fifty cents a pound."

"Cotton pickers ate at the meat markets because they weren't allowed in restaurants," said Joe Capello, the manager of City Market in Luling. "They bought their meat out of the back door and then they sat on the ground in the parking lot and ate it right there."

From the end of the Civil War until the Great Depression, the pickers were mostly Hispanics. But in 1930, Herbert Hoover's secretary of labor, William N. Doak, began deporting illegal aliens. Federal immigration authorities rounded up 82,400 Hispanics in the American Southwest and "repatriated" them to Mexico in the hopes of relieving unemployment for American citizens.

For a few years during the worst of the Depression, Okies, busted farmers, and other whites joined blacks and Hispanics in the cotton fields. And in the towns where they picked cotton, the poor whites were treated with the same disdain. In his book *The White Scourge: Mexicans, Blacks, and Poor Whites in Texas Cotton Culture*, author Neil Foley explains how the cotton culture made the people on the lowest rung of its economic ladder the untouchables of its caste system, regardless of skin color.

"Barbecue joints were on the wrong side of the tracks in those days," said Vencil Mares at his bar, the Taylor Cafe. "You didn't see women or children hanging around South Side Market in Elgin. And this place was even worse. I used to break up a knife fight in here almost every night. It didn't bother me a bit in those days. I had just come back from the Normandy invasion!"

"Cotton picking season lasted for six weeks," Edgar Black Jr., of Black's Barbecue in Lockhart, told me. Picking began in Lockhart in late July or early August and ended on September 16, Mexican

Independence Day. "And all during that time there were hundreds of cotton pickers around the square every day. They started coming in the minute we opened at 7 A.M., and they kept coming until we closed. We served nothing but beef and sausage on butcher paper with crackers on the side. That was it. We didn't have time for anything else. Sausage was a dime, three rings for a quarter."

During the harvest season, gas stations, beer halls, and anybody with a smoker got into the barbecue business. Taylor, a cotton shipping center, had a high concentration of barbecue joints. Louie Mueller's, which began as a grocery store, and Taylor Cafe, which opened in 1948 as a beer joint, are still two of the state's most famous.

In the 1990s, South Side Market in Elgin and Kreuz Market in Lockhart, two Texas barbecue institutions that built their reputations as rough-and-

tumble joints in the days of the cotton pickers, left their original buildings and moved into pleasantly decorated new restaurants. There's nothing wrong with Texas barbecue evolving into a wholesome family business. But hopefully, we will always remember our roots.

Texas barbecue traditions, like using a sheet of butcher paper for a plate, eating without utensils, or wrapping smoked meat in plain white bread are frowned upon by polite society. Few people understand these odd practices anymore, and even fewer remember that they trace their origins to the days when the cotton pickers came to town.

The recipes in this chapter include some of the cotton pickers' old favorites, along with some modern sandwiches that recall the innovative ways in which intinerant farm workers once turned the simplest ingredients into satisfying meals.

Vencil Mares
THE TAYLOR CAFE

Vencil Mares is the dean of Central Texas pit bosses. He began his barbecue career at the original location of South Side Market in downtown Elgin, where he learned how to make Elgin sausage. Mares opened the Taylor Cafe in 1948. The Taylor Cafe hasn't changed any since then; the place still has two bars and two jukeboxes—a leftover from the days of segregation.

Vencil Mares' Bohunk Sausage

VENCIL MARES OF THE TAYLOR CAFE IN TAYLOR learned how to make sausage at South Side Market in Elgin. He started working there in 1946. This is his own sausage recipe, and since he's a Bohemian Czech, he calls it Bohunk sausage.

6 pounds beef rump roast or beef trimmings
4 pounds fatty Boston butt pork roast
$1/4$ cup salt
3 tablespoons coarsely ground black pepper
Medium hog casings (available at butcher shops)

Coarsely grind the beef rump and pork butt together through the $1/4$-inch plate of a meat grinder. In a large bowl, mix the ground meat with the salt and pepper. Knead the mixture with your hands until everything is well blended.

In a small skillet, heat a little oil. Form a meatball-sized piece of the mixture into a small patty, and fry it. Taste for seasonings, and adjust to your taste.

Soak the hog casings in lukewarm water. Stuff the meat mixture into the hog casings with a sausage stuffer or a pastry bag, and tie into 4- to 6-inch links. The sausage will keep for 3 to 4 days refrigerated, and up to 2 months frozen.

When you're ready to cook the sausages, set up your smoker for indirect heat with a water pan. Sear the links over hot coals for 3 minutes on each side, or until nicely brown. Move them to indirect heat over a drip pan and smoke for 30 minutes, or until cooked through.

MAKES 10 POUNDS

Variation: Vencil's Turkey Sausage. Grind 8 pounds of boneless turkey and 2 pounds of fatty pork, and proceed with the recipe.

Vencil's Slow Beans

DON'T BE IN A RUSH TO COOK BEANS, VENCIL MARES advises. They taste best when they are cooked very slowly. A crockpot is really the perfect cooking vessel for home-cooked pintos.

2 cups dried pinto beans
$1/2$ onion, finely chopped
1 tablespoon chili powder
1 teaspoon ground black pepper
1 cup finely chopped bacon
1 teaspoon salt, or more to taste

Sort the beans to remove any stones or grit. Rinse in a colander and place the beans in a crockpot with 6 cups of water. Add the onion, chili powder, pepper, bacon, and salt.

Cook on high for 2 hours. Stir. Turn to low and allow to simmer for 8 hours or overnight. Add more water as needed.

MAKES ABOUT 6 CUPS

Variation: Beans and Sausage. Vencil Mares serves a bowl of these beans topped with sliced Bohunk sausage and a little chopped onion at the Taylor Cafe. You can spike the beans with hot sauce if you like.

Elgin Hot Guts

There's a bottle of hot sauce on the table at almost every old meat market—even the ones that refuse to serve barbecue sauce. Lots of people wonder why. "It's to heat up the sausage," Bryan Bracewell, a third-generation barbecue man, explains.

The most famous barbecue sausage in Texas is Elgin sausage, or "Elgin hot guts" as the old-timers called it. (Elgin should be pronounced EL-ghin.) This spicy sausage originated at the Southside Market, one of the oldest barbecue operations in the state. The original meat market location in downtown Elgin opened in 1886. In 1992, Southside Market moved to a larger, cleaner location out on the highway. They also toned down the spiciness of the sausage.

"Elgin hot guts were really spicy. We wanted to appeal to families," Bracewell says. "So over the years, we've cut way back on the cayenne." Texas barbecue sausage isn't as hot as it used to be in the good old days.

And that's why they put hot sauce on every table.

Buster's H-Bomb

TIM COOK OF BUSTER'S BARBECUE ON FM 620 OUTSIDE OF AUSTIN INVENTED this popular jalapeño-stuffed boneless pork-shoulder sandwich. Each slice of pork has a bull's-eye of pepper and garlic in the middle. "They call the baseball-sized hunks of boneless pork shoulder I use 'cushion meat' in the food business. It's used by Chinese restaurants a lot," Tim says. If you can't find boneless pork shoulder, try the variation with pork tenderloin called the Achiote A-Bomb (page 196).

3 cloves garlic
1 jalapeño
1-pound piece of boneless pork shoulder
3 tablespoons Rockney Terry's Pork Rub (page 63)
Sandwich fixin's:
    Sandwich rolls
    Pickle slices
    Onion slices
    Heated barbecue sauce

Smash the garlic cloves with the flat side of a knife until they are shredded. Cut the stem and tip off the jalapeño to form a tube. Slit the pepper lengthwise and, without breaking it in two, gently remove the seeds. (A fingernail works best, but remember to scrub it immediately.) Lightly stuff the hollow pepper tube with crushed garlic.

With a knife sharpening steel (or a similar tool), make a tunnel in the middle of the pork in the same direction as the grain of the meat. Widen the hole with your finger. Now gently insert the stuffed pepper into the tunnel. Secure by running a toothpick through the meat and into the pepper at each end. Roll the stuffed pork in the pork rub.

Set up your smoker for indirect heat with a water pan. Use wood chips, chunks, or logs, and keep up a good level of smoke. Maintain a temperature between 275° and 325°F.

Allow the pork to smoke for 2 hours, rotating it to expose all sides to the heat. Continue cooking until the pork reaches an internal temperature of around 155°F for medium. Allow the meat to rest for 15 minutes before slicing. After resting, it should reach 160°F (The USDA recommends 170°F.)

Slice the pork across the grain to produce slices with a bull's-eye of pepper and garlic in the middle. Serve fanned across a serving platter with sandwich fixin's.

MAKES 4 SANDWICHES

The Rafter-L Special

THE RAFTER-L WAS A TINY BARBECUE SHACK IN SONORA THAT WENT OUT OF business. They used to make one of my favorite brisket sandwiches, which they called the Rafter-L Special. Here's the way I remember it.

1 hamburger bun or kaiser roll
$^1/_4$ cup barbecue sauce of your choice
5 slices barbecued brisket
1 Anaheim chile, roasted, seeded, and cut into strips
2 slices Monterey Jack cheese

Split the bun and spread each half with barbecue sauce. Put the brisket on the bottom half and top with green chile and cheese. Place both halves in a toaster oven or under a broiler until the cheese melts. Serve immediately.

MAKES 1 SANDWICH

Railhead's Barbecued Bologna Sandwiches

I THOUGHT THIS SOUNDED LIKE A HORRIBLE IDEA UNTIL I TRIED IT. BARBECUED bologna on a bun tastes almost exactly like grilled hot dogs. Be sure to use the rindless "jumbo" bologna for this recipe. The slice should be as big around as the hamburger bun.

1 pound whole bologna (large size)
4 hamburger rolls
Barbecue sauce of your choice
1/2 cup chopped onion
8 slices dill pickle

Set up your smoker for indirect heat with a water pan. Use wood chips, chunks, or logs, and keep up a good level of smoke. Maintain a temperature between 250° and 300°F.

Smoke the bologna for an hour over indirect heat. It should have a little char on the edges and swell until it's about to burst. Split the hamburger rolls and toast them over the fire or in a toaster oven. Spread each half with barbecue sauce.

Cut the bologna into 4 thick slices, and place each on the bottom half of a roll. Top with onions and pickles. At the Railhead, they serve these sandwiches with hot French fries and cold beer.

MAKES 4 SANDWICHES

Black's Simple Slaw

WHEN THEY FINALLY STARTED SERVING SIDE DISHES at Black's Barbecue in Lockhart, they vowed to keep them as simple as possible. Here's their easy recipe for cole slaw.

$^{1}/_{2}$ cup olive oil
$^{1}/_{4}$ cup white vinegar
1 teaspoon salt
1 teaspoon ground black pepper
1 teaspoon celery seed
1 teaspoon celery salt
1 teaspoon sugar
1 teaspoon mustard
1 medium head green cabbage, shredded

Combine the oil, vinegar, salt, pepper, celery seed, celery salt, sugar, and mustard. Toss with the cabbage until well mixed. Allow to mellow in the refrigerator overnight.

MAKES ABOUT 8 CUPS

LEGENDS

How to Eat Sausage

The cotton pickers' habit of eating smoked meat with whatever they could find on the shelves of a grocery store gave us the practice of making sandwiches out of white bread, tortillas, hamburger buns, and crackers. Here are a few quick tips for making barbecued sausage sandwiches.

Sausage Wrap Wrap a flour tortilla or a slice of white bread around a link of barbecued sausage. Spread a little barbecue sauce on the sausage and sprinkle with chopped onions, if desired.

Sausage Crackers Slice a sausage into rounds and put each slice on a saltine. Sprinkle with Louisiana-style hot-pepper sauce and top with a 1-inch square of raw onion.

Sausage on a Bun Cut a link of sausage in half, and then slice the sausage halves lengthwise. Split a hamburger bun or kaiser roll, toast the halves, and spread each with the barbecue sauce of your choice. Line up the sausage slices on the bottom of the bun, and top with pickles and onions.

Sausage smoking at the Gonzales Food Market.

Laura Novosad

NOVOSAD MARKET, HALLETSVILLE

Novosad is a Czech name, and Halletsville is a Czech town. "My dad served barbecue on butcher paper without any sides, but when my wife, Laura, got into the business, we started

making beans and slaw," Nathan Novosad said from behind the counter of Novosad Market in Halletsville.

In the old days, the back of the meat market was a place where farm workers and oil-field roughnecks could eat in their dirty coveralls. They didn't have to get cleaned up as they would at a restaurant. The men were surprised when Laura showed up.

"I freaked people out when I first started working here," Laura giggled. "First a woman and then side dishes." Cold canned peaches were the only side dish served with smoked meat before Laura took over. "It's a tradition around here to eat cold canned peaches with barbecue in the summer. I tried to switch from peaches in heavy syrup to fancy homemade ones, but everybody got upset," Laura remembers.

"Some things you just can't change."

Laura Novosad's Confetti Slaw

"I CAN'T STAND SWEET COLE SLAW," Laura Novosad told me. "So I came up with this recipe. It looks real pretty with all the colors. Beans and cole slaw have gone over pretty well here at Novosad's. But we still get a lot of requests for canned peaches."

1 head green cabbage
1/2 head red cabbage
3 large carrots
1 cup Wishbone Italian dressing
    (or the Italian dressing of your choice)

Shred the cabbage and carrots and combine in a large bowl with the Italian dressing. Allow to marinate for 1 hour before serving. Serve with any kind of barbecue, and canned peaches.
MAKES 8 CUPS

Novosad's Pork Steaks

PORK STEAKS ARE ACTUALLY SLICES OF PORK SHOULDER (BOSTON BUTT), BUT don't buy a bone-in Boston butt roast thinking you're going to slice it at home— you'd need a band saw to get through the bone. Ask the butcher to slice it for you.

1 tablespoon salt
1 teaspoon ground black pepper
$^1\!/_2$ teaspoon ground sage
$^1\!/_2$ teaspoon ground bay leaf
2 pounds pork steak

Combine the seasonings and sprinkle on the pork steaks, rubbing them into the meat well.

Set up your smoker for indirect heat with a water pan. Use wood chips, chunks, or logs, and keep up a good level of smoke. Maintain a temperature between 225° and 275°F.

Place the pork in the smoker. It should take 4 to 5 hours. The meat is done when it pulls easily away from the bone, but don't worry about overcooking it. It will just keep getting better. An internal temperature of around 170°F is perfect. (This is also the USDA recommended temperature.)

SERVES 4

TENDER BONES

The Black Urban Influence

Bobby Lewis serves up barbecue and
the blues at his nightclub, Miss Ann's
Playpen, in Houston's Third Ward.

A FTER EMANCIPATION, African-Americans from East Texas and the rest of the South gravitated to large cities. In every city of size, they established at least one out-post of Southern-style barbecue. Many of these black urban barbecue joints were justly famous for their ribs. A few of them have become legendary insti-tutions that are considered treasures by their hometowns.

Miller's in San Antonio was one of the best-loved barbecue joints in the state for many years. Founder Harvey Miller grew up in the farm town of Floresville. He started Miller's Bar-B-Q in the back of his house in San Antonio in 1941. He began selling barbecue sand-wiches for fifteen cents apiece, plates for a quarter. His daughters Myrtle and Bernice kept the business going until 1990. Miller's Bar-B-Q was never listed in the Yellow Pages and never advertised, but it attracted all races, classes, and age groups to an obscure suburban backyard for fifty years. *The Washington Post, Texas Monthly*, and other publications took note.

The business operated in violation of zoning and health department regulations, but the inspectors told the Millers that the barbecue joint was too

NO
SMOKING
WE HAVE
ENOUGH

Myrtle Miller Johnson serving ribs
in 1990. Myrtle ordered that
Miller's Barbecue in San Antonio
be torn down upon her death so
that no one could give the family a
bad name with inferior barbecue.

important to the city of San Antonio to write any citations. The Millers were famous for their ribs and for their secret-recipe barbecue sauce. "Everybody wants the secret of my famous barbecue sauce," Myrtle told an interviewer in 1990 when the place closed. "People have offered to buy the recipe, and I've never been tempted to sell it. We worked on it together, Mama, Daddy . . . and I."

Myrtle Miller Johnson died in 1999 at the age of ninety-six. She took the barbecue sauce recipe to her grave.

Sam's on East 12th Street in Austin was a favorite of the blues guitarist Stevie Ray Vaughan and is still popular with the late-night music crowd. Unlike the old meat markets out in the country, which often sell out at noon and close up before five, urban barbecue joints like Sam's are hopping at three o'clock in the morning. Sam Mays, who was born in Round Rock, opened Sam's in 1978. Son Willie and daughter Wanda are in charge these days. When Sam's burned down in 1993, the entire community pitched in to rebuild the place. Volunteers donated time, money, and materials with no strings attached—just to keep Sam's in business.

Everybody cooks ribs these days, and all kinds of techniques come in and out of style. But we can thank legendary black barbecue men like Harvey Miller and Sam Mays for making smoky "bones" such a big deal in Texas.

Drexler's Ribs

THE OLD BARBECUE PIT ON DOWLING in Houston that is now called Drexler's has a remarkable pedigree. The pit was built by Harry Green in 1952. Green sold the place to one of his cooks, an old-timer named Tom Prevost. Prevost passed it on to his nephew, James Drexler (brother of Houston Rockets basketball star Clyde Drexler). James has been smoking ribs on the old pit now for twenty-seven years. Here's his recipe for smoking pork ribs at home.

1 rack pork spareribs (under 3¹/₂ pounds)
¹/₄ cup paprika
2 tablespoons salt
2 tablespoons sugar
1 tablespoon garlic powder
1 tablespoon onion powder

Rinse the ribs, then dry them. Sprinkle the seasonings on both sides and rub them in.

Set up your smoker for indirect heat with a water pan. Use wood chips, chunks, or logs, and keep up a good level of smoke. Maintain a temperature between 250° and 300°F. Place the ribs on the smoker, bone-side down, as far away from the fire as possible. Cook for 3 to 3¹/₂ hours, or until a toothpick goes through easily when inserted between the bones.

Sit back, drink a beer, and don't be in a rush. They'll get very tender if you give them enough time.

SERVES 2 TO 4

LEGENDS

James Drexler

DREXLER'S, HOUSTON

James Drexler suggests that after you trim your pork ribs, you cook the trimmings seperately. First of all, it would be a crime to throw away all that meat, and second, it's an old East Texas tradition. The breastbone, back flap, and bottom pieces are cooked by themselves and set aside at Drexler's. These odd scraps of cooked meat are called "regulars". (The word is probably a corruption of "irregulars.")

"In the old days, people who didn't have enough money to buy barbecue would come to the back door and we'd sell them all the little burnt ends and scraps of meat we had left over," James remembers. "They called them the 'regulars. We still have customers who ask for them today, not because they're poor, but because they taste so good. Only people who have been eating barbecue for a long time know to ask for 'regulars."

When you barbecue ribs at home, make yourself a special "cook's treat." Trim the ribs, season the scraps with rib rub, and smoke them along with the ribs. The 'regulars will be done much quicker than the rest of the rack, so you'll have something to munch on while you're cooking.

Sonny Bryan's Rib Sandwiches

SONNY BRYAN'S IN DALLAS MADE THE RIB SANDWICH FAMOUS. ONLY VERY tender East Texas–style ribs are soft enough to make sandwiches. The legendary Sonny Bryan has passed away, and his barbecue joints in Dallas aren't what they used to be. But the rib sandwich lives on.

1 rack well-cooked East Texas ribs
4 or 5 hamburger buns
1 cup barbecue sauce of your choice
Onion slices
Pickle slices

Carve the ribs and pull the meat off the bones. Chop the meat, discarding any tough pieces. Dip the inside of the bottom half of each hamburger bun in the bar-becue sauce. Pile the meat on the buns and top with onion and pickle slices. Add additional sauce to the top halves of the buns. Serve immediately.

MAKES 4 OR 5 SANDWICHES

Dozier's Crispy Grilled Ribs

BILLY PFEFFER IS FIFTY-THREE, AND HE HAS BEEN THE PIT BOSS AT DOZIER'S
Grocery since he was eighteen. Scott Evans and his brother, Smedley, bought the
old grocery store and meat market from the Dozier brothers in 1985. Billy Pfeffer
came along with the store. Here's how Billy Pfeffer cooks ribs.

2 cups white vinegar
2 cups vegetable oil
1 rack 3^1/$_2$ and down pork spareribs (under 3^1/$_2$ pounds)
3 tablespoons Billy Pfeffer's Dry Rub (recipe follows)
Barbecue sauce of your choice (optional)

Combine the vinegar and oil in a mixing bowl. Rinse the ribs and pat them dry.
Season both sides of the ribs with the dry rub.

Set up your smoker for direct heat. When the coals are gray, spread them out
and place the ribs on a grill at least 18 inches above the coals. Cook for 20 minutes,
mop with the oil and vinegar mixture, and then flip the ribs over and cook the other
side. Light more coals in a chimney starter and replenish the fire after 1 hour.
Continue flipping and mopping for roughly 2 hours, or until tender. Serve with
barbecue sauce if desired.

SERVES 2 TO 4

Billy Pfeffer's Dry Rub

3 tablespoons salt
3 tablespoons good paprika
1 tablespoon ground black pepper
1 tablespoon cayenne

Combine all ingredients and store in a shaker bottle.

MAKES ABOUT ^{1}/$_2$ CUP.

LBJ and Hubert Humphrey dig into the ribs at a victory celebration on the LBJ ranch in 1964.

Rib Terminology

3¹/₂ and down Most Texas barbecue joints and all top cook-off competitors insist on 3¹/₂ and down pork spareribs. This is a meat industry classification that refers to the weight of the ribs (under 3¹/₂ pounds). Due to the increasing demand for ribs, these choice spareribs are getting harder and harder to find.

To get your hands on some 3¹/₂ and down ribs, you'll need to find a real butcher. Don't confuse the average meat-counter attendant at the supermarket with a butcher. When I asked for 3¹/₂ and down ribs at one supermarket, the guy behind the scales offered to cut a 5-pound slab in half! Discount stores sometimes sell 3¹/₂ and down ribs in cases and three-packs. But your best bet is to order them from a quality meat market or the head butcher at a good grocery store.

Baby back ribs These are the very tender, but very expensive, under 2-pound racks of ribs. They are favored in grilling recipes because they cook very quickly. You can substitute baby backs for 3¹/₂ and downs in any of these recipes. Just decrease the cooking time a little.

4 and up These giant racks of ribs (4 pounds and up) come from larger hogs and are not the best for barbecuing. They take forever to cook, and never do get as tender as the smaller sizes. If you settle for the bigger racks, you're going to have to make some compromises in the cooking.

Falls County Easy Pork Ribs

ROCKNEY TERRY AND THE FALLS COUNTY BARBE-cue cook-off team won the Overall trophy at the 1996 Houston Livestock Show and Rodeo World Championship Barbecue Cook-Off. Rockney gave me this easy recipe for pork ribs. Wrapping the ribs in aluminum foil after a couple of hours of smoking is a quick way to produce the falling-apart texture. Terry likes his ribs without sauce. "It's like a good steak. Who needs sauce?" he says.

1 tablespoon salt
1 tablespoon coarsely ground black pepper
1 tablespoon sugar
1 teaspoon garlic powder
1 rack 3¹/₂ and down pork spareribs (under 3¹/₂ pounds)
Barbecue sauce of your choice (optional)

Combine the salt, pepper, sugar, and garlic powder in a shaker. Rinse the ribs, then dry them. Season both sides with the seasoning mix and rub it in.

Set up your smoker for indirect heat. Use wood chips, chunks, or logs, and keep up a good level of smoke. Maintain a temperature between 250° and 300°F. Place the ribs on the smoker, bone-side down, as far away from the fire as possible. Cook for 2 to 2¹/₂ hours, or until the ribs are a nice color. Wrap the ribs in aluminum foil and continue cooking another hour or until they're falling-apart tender. Serve with barbecue sauce, if desired.

SERVES 2 TO 4

Variation: 4 and Ups. This recipe will also work well on larger rib racks, but you'll need to increase the cooking time to 3¹/₂ to 4 hours on the smoker and at least 2 hours in the foil.

Art Blondin's Chipotle-Marinated Ribs

COOK-OFF COMPETITOR AND BARBECUE JOINT owner Art Blondin is a rib specialist. At Artz Rib House in Austin, he serves every size and shape of ribs imaginable. Here's his favorite recipe for baby back ribs.

1 rack baby back ribs

Art's Chipotle Marinade:
$^1/_4$ cup red wine
$^1/_4$ cup honey
$^1/_4$ cup Búfalo brand chipotle sauce or
    Chipotle Ketchup (page 88)
$^1/_4$ cup canola oil
Salt and ground black pepper to taste

Rinse off the ribs. Combine the marinade ingredients and mix well. Cover the ribs with marinade in a plastic bag or flat plastic container, and marinate for 1 to 2 hours at room temperature or overnight in the refrigerator. (It's okay to cut the rack in half if necessary.)

Set up your smoker for indirect heat. Use wood chips, chunks, or logs, and keep up a good level of smoke. Maintain a temperature between 200° and 225°F. Place the ribs on the smoker, bone-side down, as far away from the fire as possible. Cook for 3 to $3^1/_2$ hours. The ribs are ready when a toothpick goes through easily when inserted between the bones.

SERVES 2 TO 3

St. Louis cut To trim a rack of ribs St. Louis style, you cut off the breastbone, back flap, and lower ribs to produce a squared-up rack that fits nicely on the grill (see fig. 1 and 2). The breastbone is connected to the top few ribs—it runs north and south while the ribs run east and west. Removing it also makes carving at the table much easier.

Skinning your ribs There is a membrane on the bone side of a rack of ribs that many barbecuers like to remove. Some argue that this process speeds cooking time, some say it makes the ribs more tender. When cooking 4 and ups with a braising liquid, it's definitely a good idea to remove the skin because it allows the steam to penetrate the meat.

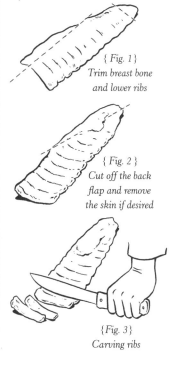

{ Fig. 1 }
*Trim breast bone
and lower ribs*

{ Fig. 2 }
*Cut off the back
flap and remove
the skin if desired*

{Fig. 3}
Carving ribs

Broasted 4 and Ups

YOU CAN ALSO USE A MARINADE AS A BRAISING liquid to tenderize tough 4 and ups before smoking. Broasting is a combination of braising and roasting.

1 rack 4 and up ribs, 4 to 5 pounds
1 cup red wine
$1/4$ cup Búfalo brand chipotle sauce or
    Chipotle Ketchup (page 88)
1 cup water
$1/2$ cup canola oil
Salt and ground black pepper to taste

    Preheat the oven to 350°F. Rinse the ribs, trim the rack "St. Louis" style (see page 181), and remove the skin (see page 181). Combine the wine, chipotle sauce, water, oil, salt, and pepper. Place the rack bone-side down in a shallow baking pan and pour the wine mixture around it. The top of the ribs should be above the liquid so they steam rather than boil. Bake for 1 hour. Remove the ribs from the pan and then proceed with any rib recipe that calls for $3^{1}/2$ and downs.
SERVES 3 TO 4

Variations: Rosemary Garlic Broasted Ribs. Use 1 cup water, 1 cup wine, 3 sprigs rosemary, and 5 cloves crushed garlic for the broasting liquid.

LEGENDS

New Zion Missionary Baptist Church Barbecue

Howard Rivers lifts the lid of the steel barbecue pit and sticks a huge fork into a slab of ribs. You know when they're done because the fork slides through easy, he tells me.

The barbecue pit is mounted on a trailer, but both tires are flat. The pit evidently isn't going anywhere. Neither is Howard Rivers. Sitting around, shooting the breeze with the boys on the front porch of the New Zion Missionary Baptist Church Barbecue in Huntsville looks like a fine way to spend the afternoon. The scene reminds me more of a barbecue in my backyard than the hustle and bustle of a restaurant (except that there isn't any beer). I pull up a chair anyway and join a conversation about this year's pecan harvest. Barbecue may not actually be a religion in Texas, but the two institutions are closely associated.

New Zion Ribs

AT NEW ZION MISSIONARY BAPTIST CHURCH barbecue in Huntsville, they cook ribs on the smoker for three hours and then hold the hot ribs a dozen racks at a time in a large ice chest. The ice chest keeps the ribs hot and traps the steam so they get more tender. You can accomplish the same thing by dousing the ribs with barbecue sauce and wrapping them in aluminum foil. For information on ordering Tex-Joy Barb-B-Q Seasoning, see "Online and Mail Order Sources" on page 252.

1 rack 3½ and down pork spareribs (under 3½ pounds)
Tex-Joy Bar-B-Q Seasoning (or the dry rub of your choice)
Barbecue sauce of your choice, heated

Rinse the ribs to remove any blood. Season both sides with the dry rub, wrap them in plastic wrap, and put them in the refrigerator overnight.

Set up your smoker for indirect heat. Use wood chips, chunks, or logs, and keep up a good level of smoke. Maintain a temperature between 250° and 300°F. Place the ribs on the smoker, bone-side down, as far away from the fire as possible Cook for 3 to 3½ hours, turning every hour at first, then every half hour.

Cut the rack in half. Brush the ribs with heated barbecue sauce. (Do not use cold sauce!) Wrap with aluminum foil and return to the smoker for 15 minutes, turning once. Allow the ribs to sit for at least another 15 minutes before serving, or until they're falling-apart tender.

SERVES 2 TO 4

Variation: 4 and Ups. For larger ribs, increase the cooking time on the smoker to 4 hours, then coat with barbecue sauce, wrap in foil, and continue cooking for another hour. Or place the foil-wrapped ribs in a roasting pan and put them in the oven for an hour or until falling-apart tender (the pan keeps the foil from tearing).

East Texas camp meetings organized by travelling preachers always featured free barbecue. The sponsors of the meeting would donate sheep, goats, and cattle, and the smell of the meat cooking would attract "joiners" from all around. The preaching, testifying, and singing of hymns would continue for as long as the barbecue held out.

The Texas camp-meeting barbecue style is still going strong here at Mount Zion Missionary Baptist. Sitting down with the congregation in the funky little church hall is an experience every true barbecue believer should have at least once. It's like a pilgrimage to Mecca.

The barbecue began in 1981 when Sister Ward organized a barbecue dinner in the church hall as a fund-raiser. It was such a success that they did it again a week later, and pretty soon it just became a permanent thing every Wednesday through Saturday. The down-home cooking and good-hearted volunteers make this a wonderful scene. It may not be enough to convert you, but I would gladly sit through a three-hour sermon if I knew this kind of homemade barbecue was waiting for me at the end.

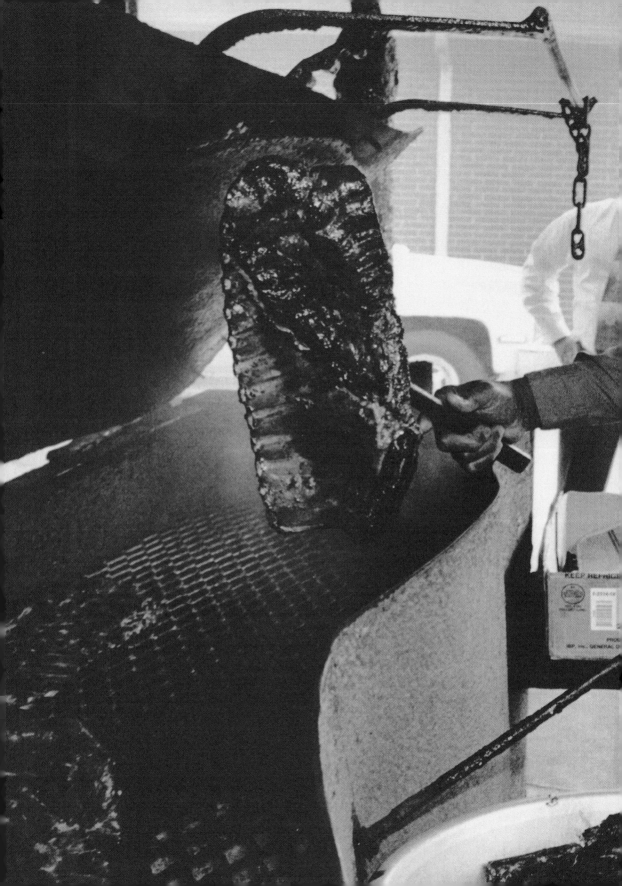

Pit boss Howard Rivers checks a slab of ribs at New Zion Missionary Baptist Church Barbecue in Huntsville.

BARBACOA AND BORRACHO BEANS

Down in South Texas

Armando Vera and his father cook *barbacoa* (cow heads) the old-fashioned way in a brick pit at Vera's backyard barbecue in Brownsville.

LARGE PERCENTAGE of the state's top pit bosses are Tejanos, or Mexican-Texans. You'll find the same brisket, ribs, and sausage in Tejano barbecue joints that you'll find in the rest of the state, but there is one kind of legendary Texas barbecue that is uniquely Tejano—*barbacoa*.

Barbacoa is the Spanish word from which the English word "barbecue" is derived. In Central Mexico, *barbacoa* is lamb or goat meat wrapped in maguey leaves and roasted on hot coals, but it means something different in Texas. On the cattle ranches along the Mexican border, Mexican ranch hands were given part of their pay in less desirable cuts of beef, such as the head and offal. The Mexican vaqueros adapted the interior Mexican style of *barbacoa* to roast the cow heads. They wrapped the heads in maguey leaves or later in aluminum foil and canvas and buried them in earthen pits with hot coals.

Barbacoa is still a popular tradition in Texas, but the cooking methods have changed. There are reportedly two or three restaurants in the state that have been granted grandfather status by the county health department for their old brick-lined, dirt floor *barbacoa* pits, but the practice won't last much longer.

"No, we don't cook it in the ground anymore," Paula Luna told me at Johnny's BBQ in Pharr, down in the Lower Rio Grande Valley one Sunday morning. "The health department won't let us. But I grew up in Los Ebanos, and we still do it that way down there for our family." Los Ebanos ("the ebony trees" in Spanish) is a tiny border town famous for having the last rope-pulled ferry across the Rio Grande.

For her family in Los Ebanos, Paula seasons the cow heads, or *cabezas*, with salt and pepper and then wraps them in foil. She then puts each one in an empty ten-gallon metal lard container and puts the lid on it. Paula's brother buries the cans under a layer of dirt and builds a big fire on top. "You have to pack the earth down good. If you leave any air in there, it won't get done," she says. The fire burns through the night, and the *cabezas* are dug up in the morning.

At Johnny's Barbecue, Johnny Harper cooks his cabezas in a pit over a water bath. "You put the heads on a screen above the water and let them steam overnight," he told me. In the rest of Texas, *barbacoa* is usually made in a conventional oven with a water bath (called a *baño Maria* in Spanish) underneath the head.

I asked Johnny and Paula how to make *barbacoa* at home. "Use an electric roaster oven," Paula told me. "You know, the kind you cook turkeys in. You put some water in the bottom and cook it for about twelve hours—it stays real juicy."

If you have a weak stomach, I recommend you skip the recipes for *barbacoa* and *lengua* that follow. Skim ahead to the wonderful recipes for Achiote A-Bomb (page 196), BBQ Pork and Garlicky Guacamole Sandwiches (page 198), and the definitive recipe for slow-cooked Borracho Beans (page 204). If you aren't easily grossed out and you really want to cook *barbacoa* at home, you'll find all the gory details on the pages that follow.

Barbacoa

IT IS BOTHERSOME THAT MODERN *BARBACOA* DOESN'T INVOLVE SMOKE.
There are ways around this problem. You can smoke the cow's head in your
barbecue pit for several hours before cooking it. It is also possible to add liquid
smoke to the water in an electric roaster oven. But 99 percent of the state's
Tejanos make their *barbacoa* without any smoke.

If you live in Texas, you can usually get a cow's head at any Fiesta supermarket. Get the smallest one you can find. The bigger ones don't fit in
conventional ovens or electric roaster ovens. If you don't live in Texas, see
"Online and Mail Order Sources" on page 252 for information on
ordering *cabezas*.

1 cow head, 20 to 25 pounds, skinned and cleaned
Salt and ground black pepper to taste
Garlic powder to taste
Chili powder to taste
2 onions, peeled and cut in half
Accompaniments:
    Fresh corn tortillas
    Lime quarters
    Chopped onion
    Cilantro
    Valley Verde Sauce (page 89), Barbecued Tomato Salsa (page 90),
      or Pico de Gallo (page 91)

Ready? Take a deep breath.

The head should be skinned, with all the extraneous things (like ears)
removed. Rinse the head out with a hose. Cut out the tongue and reserve it for
making *lengua* (page 194). Sprinkle salt, pepper, garlic powder, and chili powder all
over the head. Put the head upside down (forehead down) in an 18-quart electric
roaster oven. (You may need to angle it a little to get it to fit.) Add 8 cups water,
and put the onions in the water. Cover. If the lid won't fit, cut 2 sheets of 18-inch-
wide aluminum foil long enough to cover the top of the roaster with plenty to
spare. Combine the 2 sheets by overlapping and folding them to make one
32-inch-wide piece of foil, and seal the roaster with it by tucking and folding the
foil onto the roaster pan.

Turn the roaster oven to 350°F and heat for an hour, or until the water is boiling vigorously. Reduce the heat to 250°F and allow to steam for 12 hours, or until
the cheek meat pulls away from the bone.

When the *barbacoa* is done, pull the cheek meat off, then remove the jaw bones. You'll find another large piece of meat inside. Remove any other nice chunks of meat you can find.

Cut away excess fat, blackened meat, and cartilage, but don't clean the meat too thoroughly. It is the little bits of fat and mucilage that give *barbacoa* its distinctive texture. Chop the meat and put it in a bowl. Wet the meat with some of the cooking liquid to keep it moist. You should end up with around 2 pounds of meat.

Serve immediately with fresh corn tortillas, lime quarters, chopped onion, cilantro and Valley Verde Sauce, Barbecued Tomato Salsa, or Pico de Gallo.

MAKES ABOUT 2 POUNDS, OR 6 TO 8 SERVINGS

Lengua (Tongue)

BARBACOA IS A HASSLE, BUT *LENGUA* IS JUST AS GOOD AND IT'S REALLY EASY, says Paula Luna of Johnny's BBQ. Just put the tongue in a crockpot on Saturday night and you'll have *lengua* tacos on Sunday morning.

1 beef tongue, about 1 pound
Salt and ground black pepper to taste
3 cloves garlic, minced
1 onion, cut in half
Accompaniments:
    Fresh corn tortillas
    Lime quarters
    Chopped onion
    Cilantro
    Valley Verde Sauce (page 89), Barbecued Tomato Salsa (page 90),
      or Pico de Gallo (page 91)

At 8 P.M., rinse the tongue well, season it with salt and pepper, and put it in a crockpot with water to cover. Add the garlic and onion to the water. Turn the crockpot to high. At 1 A.M., turn the tongue over and add more water if needed. Turn the crockpot down to low.

When the *lengua* is done, the skin should be hard and the meat should be soft. Put the *lengua* on a cutting board and remove and discard the skin. (It should come away easily.) Chop the meat finely.

Serve immediately with fresh corn tortillas, lime quarters, chopped onion, cilantro, and Valley Verde Sauce, Barbecued Tomato Salsa, or Pico de Gallo.

MAKES ABOUT 1 POUND, OR 3 TO 4 SERVINGS

Ray Lopez's Beef Ribs

GONZALES FOOD MARKET SELLS SOME OF THE BEST beef ribs in the state. I asked pit boss Ray Lopez what his secret was. He said, "I don't know, I just put them in a pan and smoke them for three or four hours." I didn't really understand the point of using a pan until I tried it. The grease collects in the pan and the ribs fry up crispy while they're smoking. It's a technique I plan to try on some other meats soon.

2 to 3 pounds beef short ribs
3 tablespoons dry rub of your choice
  (preferably one without sugar)

Set up your smoker for indirect heat. Use wood chips, chunks, or logs, and keep up a good level of smoke. Maintain a temperature between 270° and 325°F.

Sprinkle the dry rub on the ribs and rub it in well. Put the short ribs in a glass or metal baking pan in the smoker, close to the heat source. Smoke for 3 hours, turning often to crisp all sides. Beef ribs are done when they are falling apart.

SERVES 4

Achiote A-Bombs

THIS COLORFUL BARBECUED PORK TENDERLOIN IS RED ON THE OUTSIDE WITH A bull's-eye of jalapeño pepper and crushed garlic in the middle of every slice. The recipe is adapted from Buster's Barbecue outside of Austin, where Buster's H-Bomb was invented. If you can't find Mexican achiote paste, just use a pork rub. Select serranos that are straight, not curved.

1/2 cup achiote paste
1 cup orange juice
1 1/2 pounds pork tenderloin
10 cloves garlic
4 large serrano chiles
Sandwich fixin's:
    Sandwich rolls
    Sliced pickles
    Sliced onions
    Heated barbecue sauce

In a medium bowl, mix the achiote paste with the orange juice until it forms a smooth liquid. Pour into a plastic freezer bag and add the pork tenderloin. Put the bag in a container in the refrigerator and marinate overnight.

Smash the garlic cloves with the side of a knife blade until they are flat and shredded. Cut the stems and tips off the peppers to form tubes. Slit the peppers lengthwise and, without breaking them in two, gently remove the seeds. (A fingernail works best, but remember to scrub it immediately.) Lightly stuff the hollow pepper tubes with crushed garlic.

Remove the tenderloin from the marinade and transfer it to a cutting board. Cut off the large ragged end and the small point at the tip so you have a regular cylinder of meat. (Reserve the scraps.)

Measure the meat with peppers and cut the cylinder into pieces that are 2 or 3 peppers long. With a knife sharpening steel (or similar tool), make a tunnel in the middle of the pork pieces from one end to the other. Going slowly, as the meat grain will tend to channel the steel off to one side, continue working straight through the middle. Widen the hole with your finger. Gently insert the stuffed peppers into the tunnel so that they run the length of each piece of meat. Secure by running a toothpick through the meat and into the pepper at each end.

Set up your smoker for indirect heat. Use wood chips, chunks, or logs, and keep up a good level of smoke. Maintain a temperature between 270° and 325°F.

Allow the pork to smoke for 1¹/₂ hours, rotating it to expose all sides to the heat. Continue cooking until the pork reaches an internal temperature of around 155°F for medium. Allow the roast to rest for 15 minutes before slicing. After resting it should reach 160°F. (The USDA recommends 170°F.)

Slice the pork into ¹/₄-inch circles and serve fanned across a serving platter with sandwich fixin's.

SERVES 4

BBQ Pork and Garlicky Guacamole Sandwiches

THE GREAT THING ABOUT COOKING BARBECUE WITHOUT SAUCE IS THAT THE serving possibilities are limitless. When I barbecue a Boston butt, I usually serve sliced pork roast the first night with barbecue sauce, beans, cole slaw, and all the usual trimmings. But when it comes to the leftovers, I make all sorts of things out of it. Here, for instance, is my favorite leftover smoked pork sandwich. By crisping the leftover pork chunks in a frying pan, you turn the barbecued pork roast into something that tastes like Mexican *carnitas*.

$^1/_4$ cup olive oil
$1^1/_2$ pounds Ruthie's Pork Shoulder (page 119), chopped
Salt to taste
4 *bolillos* (small sub sandwich rolls)
1 cup Garlicky Guacamole (opposite)
2 teaspoons bottled hot-pepper sauce

In a medium skillet, heat the olive oil over high heat. Season the pork with salt and cook it in the hot oil for about 5 minutes, then reduce the heat a little.

Slice the bolillos open lengthwise, open them up, and put them on top of the pork to heat. Cook the meat for 4 to 6 more minutes, turning frequently until crisp.

Spoon $^1/_4$ cup guacamole onto each warm roll. Divide the pork among the rolls and top each with $^1/_2$ teaspoon hot-pepper sauce.

SERVES 4

Garlicky Guacamole

MAKE THIS BATCH OF GUACAMOLE SUPER GARLICKY IF YOU'RE GOING TO USE it on barbecued pork sandwiches. You may need to buy your avocados in advance and leave them on the windowsill until they soften a little. Don't bother trying to make guacamole with firm avocados. And don't buy squishy ones—they'll be black inside.

3 serrano chiles, chopped
1 onion, diced
4 cloves garlic, minced, or more to taste
1 1/2 tablespoons fresh lemon juice
3 ripe avocados, pitted and peeled
1/2 cup chopped cilantro
Salt to taste

Combine the ingredients in a mixing bowl and mash until creamy. Serve immediately. Guacamole discolors quickly, so don't try to refrigerate it too long.

MAKES 2 TO 2 1/2 CUPS

Cocinero Juan Cesares prepares
barbecue for the cowboys during
round-up on a South Texas ranch.

Potato and Black Bean Salsa Salad

THIS RECIPE FROM A NATIONAL POTATO MARKETING ORGANIZATION combines a corn and black bean salsa with potatoes for a modern Latino-style potato salad.

1½ pounds (4 medium) potatoes, peeled and cut into 1-inch cubes
3 tablespoons vegetable oil
2 tablespoons bottled or fresh lime juice
1½ tablespoons hot-pepper sauce
1½ teaspoons chili powder
½ teaspoon salt
One 15-ounce can black beans, thoroughly rinsed and drained
One 7-ounce can vacuum-packed whole-kernel corn, drained
1 cup diced tomatoes
½ cup sliced scallions, including some of the green tops

In a 3-quart saucepan, cook the potatoes, covered in 2 inches of boiling water, for 10 to 12 minutes, just until tender. Drain and cool.

Meanwhile, in a large bowl, combine the oil, lime juice, hot-pepper sauce, chili powder, and salt.

Add the potatoes, beans, corn, tomatoes, and scallions. Toss gently to mix thoroughly. Allow to mellow in the refrigerator for at least an hour before serving.
SERVES 6

Gonzales Food Market Macaroni Salad

SLIGHTLY SWEET MACARONI SALAD WITH RAISINS IS a favorite at the old Food Market in Gonzales.

8 ounces elbow macaroni
$^1/_2$ cup chopped onion
$^1/_2$ cup chopped celery
2 carrots, grated
$^1/_4$ cup raisins
1 cup mayonnaise
Salt and ground black pepper to taste

Cook the elbow macaroni until tender. Rinse with cold water in a colander and drain well.

In a large bowl, combine the cooked macaroni with the onion, celery, carrots, raisins, and mayonnaise, and season with salt and pepper. Place in the refrigerator until well chilled.

SERVES 4

LEGENDS

Pachanga

"Pachanga" is a South Texas slang term for an outdoor gathering that includes barbecue, music, and comraderie. At election time, politicians hold pachangas to win votes.

Borracho Beans

BORRACHO MEANS DRUNK, AND IT REFERS TO THE BEER IN THE COOKING liquid. If you're cooking beans and pork roast at the same time, you can use the fatty pieces of pork that you remove while carving to add flavor to the beans. Otherwise, use some bacon.

2 cups dried pinto beans
4 cups water
1 can beer
1 clove garlic, minced
1/2 onion, finely chopped
3 sprigs epazote (optional)
1 tablespoon guajillo chile powder (ground chiles)
1/2 teaspoon ground cumin
1 cup finely chopped fatty pork scraps or bacon
One 15-ounce can of tomatoes, chopped
1 teaspoon salt, or more to taste

Sort the beans to remove any stones or grit. Rinse the beans in a colander and place in a large pan with the water and beer. Add the garlic, onion, epazote (if using), chile powder, cumin, pork or bacon, tomatoes, and salt.

Boil the beans for an hour and then reduce to a simmer and cook over very low heat until soft (12 hours in a crockpot or other slow cooker works best). Keep the level of the broth a good inch or so above the beans, and add more water as needed. Serve with broth in a bowl as a side dish.

MAKES ABOUT 6 CUPS

Pickled Jalapeños

THESE "TEXAS PICKLES" ARE EASY TO MAKE. PUT A BIG JAR UP IN THE FALL when peppers flood the supermarkets, and they should last you a good while.

30 jalapeños (about $^3/_4$ pound)
2 carrots, peeled and cut on the diagonal (about $^1/_3$ pound)
1 onion, peeled and cut into wedges, stem end to root end
5 cups white vinegar
1 teaspoon pickling salt

Place the jalapeños, carrots, and onion in a large bowl.

Pour the vinegar into a saucepan and add the salt. Heat to boiling. Pour the hot liquid over the jalapeños, stir to combine the ingredients, and place a plate on top of the peppers to keep them submerged in the hot liquid. Let cool to room temperature.

Transfer the mixture to two clean 2-quart nonreactive containers with lids. Set aside in the refrigerator for 24 hours before serving.

MAKES 3 TO 4 QUARTS

SMOKING BEEF

Clods, Sirloins, and Briskets

Smoked briskets ready for slicing
at House Park Barbecue in Austin

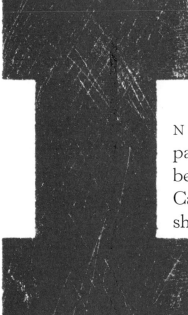

IN THE 1950S AND 1960S, MEAT packing, once a local business, became a national industry. Cattle raised on ranches were shipped off and fattened on feed-lots. Texas meat markets didn't slaughter their own cattle anymore. For the first time, barbecue joints weren't obliged to cook the chuck, shoulder, and other forequarter cuts left over from their meat cases—they were free to order the cuts of their choice from packing houses.

Some old meat markets began to barbecue shoulder clod, some cowboy barbecue restaurants in West Texas began to feature sirloin. But what most Texas barbecue joints ordered was untrimmed brisket.

Brisket is well suited to the restaurant business. It is relatively cheap, and provides a uniform slice of meat to each customer. Lately, brisket has been made even more attractive by the decline in internal marbling levels of other cuts of American beef. When the low-fat food trend started seriously hurting beef sales, the cattle industry called for a change in the way that beef was being graded. In 1987, USDA Good, the third class of beef under Prime and Choice, was renamed USDA Select.

"Over the last twenty years, the beef industry has started feeding cattle differently in order to produce leaner beef," says Molly Patterson of the National Cattleman's Beef Association. "American beef is 27 percent leaner today than it was twenty years ago." As a result, the production of USDA Prime and Choice is down, and the internal fat content of sirloins, shoulder roasts, and other cuts of beef that can be barbecued has fallen.

"When we barbecue shoulder clod, we use USDA Choice," says Rick Schmidt, the pit boss at Kreuz Market in Lockhart. "Generally, USDA Choice is the best-quality beef for barbecuing."

For shoulder roasts, sirloin tip roasts, and other barbecued beef cuts, Black Angus, Sterling, or other branded beef has become your best bet for a good cut of meat. The branded beef programs go beyond government grading," says Molly Patterson. After the USDA issues a grade, the brand-name graders come through and stamp the meat that fits their program. What they are really doing, by and large, is taking the beef that falls within the top third of the USDA Choice category—the best beef available in the market.

Brisket is an exception. With the enormous fat cap on a packer's cut (untrimmed) brisket, you don't need as much internal marbling in the meat. "I prefer USDA Select brisket. There's too much waste fat on a Choice brisket," says Rick Schmidt.

While brisket is widely available, it is a major challenge for the home bar-becuer. Like a pot roast, brisket must be cooked for a long time to become tender. There is just no way to hurry the process up. "There is no medium-rare to this part of the steer—it is either totally cooked and edible or it's not," warns Jim Goode of Goode Company Barbecue in Houston.

Even when you follow all the recipe instructions to the letter, brisket often comes out dry. That's why it is considered the true test of barbecue skill in Texas. It's hard to mess up a pork roast, but it's easy to ruin a brisket. Before you decide to try it, I suggest you think it through carefully.

First, consider your equipment. You couldn't even fit a brisket on a small Weber, and even if you could, think of the hassle of refueling. To maintain a 250 degree fire for twelve to fifteen hours, you need to refuel at least once an hour. With a barrel or a bigger rig, you're in much better shape. The farther you can get the brisket from the fire, the better.

If you have the equipment, the next question is, "Are you going to be a pragmatist and wrap the brisket in aluminum foil after you get a nice color and smoke level, or are you going to be a purist and smoke it all the way?"

Wrapping a brisket in foil helps ensure a tender finished product. Such famous barbecue joints as Cooper's in Llano and John's Country Store in Egypt wrap theirs, so why shouldn't you?

"Because wrapping a brisket in foil ruins the smoke ring and makes the meat mushy. You will never win a

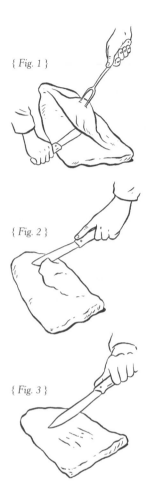

{ Fig. 1 }

{ Fig. 2 }

{ Fig. 3 }

Slicing a Brisket

Brisket has a fat side and a lean side. You don't want to separate them until the last minute because the fat keeps the meat moist. When you are ready to eat, run a knife between the lean meat on the flat bottom and the layer of fat above it (Figure 1).

There is a big piece of meat on the fat side. Carve it against the grain (Figure 2). Cut the lean side into slices carving against the grain (Figure 3) as well.

barbecue cook-off with foil-wrapped brisket," says Harley Goerlitz. If you want to see that deep red smoke ring on every slice, you'll have to tend the fire for as long as it takes.

If you wrap it in foil, are you going to keep it on the smoker or finish it in the oven? Some people say there isn't any difference. Others say the smoke still penetrates the foil. Most Texans base this decision on how hot it is outside.

When the outdoor temperature exceeds 95 degrees (as it often does in Texas for six months of the year), Texans are loath to turn on the oven. There is something perverse (not to mention expensive) about simultaneously heating and cooling your house. So finishing a foil-wrapped brisket on the smoker isn't always a culinary decision.

There are also some Texans who cook a brisket in the oven from start to finish. Benny Wade Clewis, for instance, grew up eating East Texas–style barbecue and wishes he still could. But Clewis is currently incarcerated in the Darrington Penitentiary in Rosesharon, where he is a prison cook. When he gets a chance to make a brisket these days, he makes it in the oven with liquid smoke.

"The kind you make in the oven ain't as good as the real thing," Clewis told me when I visited him in prison several years ago. "But it's as close as I'm gonna get." I asked for his recipe (see page 228) and he sent it to me in a letter.

Here are a few recipes for barbecued beef roasts and for the ultimate challenge of Texas barbecue— brisket.

The brisket recipes start with the most complicated and challenging recipes for you purists who want to try to win a trophy, and work their way down to the easiest recipe of all, the kind you just throw in the oven. Pick your level of difficulty and get after it.

When you can consistently turn out a moist and tender barbecued brisket, you have passed Texas barbecue's final exam.

John Fullilove's Rib Roast

THE BARBECUED PRIME RIB AT SMITTY'S AND KREUZ may be the most expensive barbecue in Texas. "I don't know why anybody wants to cook a brisket at home," wonders John Fullilove, the pit boss at Smitty's. "If I'm cooking at home, I'm going to get a nice cut like a sirloin or a rib roast and smoke it at 300 to 350 degrees," he says. "I'd just season it with salt and pepper, same as we do at Smitty's."

1 USDA Prime 3-bone beef rib roast, 3$^1/_2$ to 4 pounds
  (Black Angus or other USDA Choice branded beef can
  be substituted)
Salt and cracked black pepper to taste
$^1/_4$ teaspoon cayenne

Let the roast come to room temperature. Combine the salt, pepper, and cayenne and sprinkle the roast with the rub. Set up your smoker for indirect heat. Use wood chips, chunks, or logs, and keep up a good level of smoke. Maintain a temperature between 325° and 350°F (or as hot as your smoker will allow without charring the meat).

Allow the roast to smoke for 2 hours, rotating it to expose all sides to the heat. Continue cooking, checking and turning every half hour, until the roast reaches an internal temperature of around 130°F for medium-rare. Allow the roast to rest for 15 minutes before slicing. After resting, the roast should reach 135°F. (The USDA recommends 140°F.)

SERVES 6 TO 8

Beef comes first, but Texas barbecue is equally famous for its variety.

Maurice Mikeska's Tri-Tip

AT MAURICE MIKESKA'S MEAT MARKET ON MERCHANT STREET IN EL CAMPO, they don't serve brisket. The only cut of beef Mikeska's barbecues is tri-tip roast. Tri-tip, also known as triangle roast or culotte steak, is an economical cut from the bottom sirloin that includes quite a bit of internal marbling, so it stays moist.

Louis Charles Henley's All-Purpose Rub (page 118.)
1 USDA Choice beef tri-tip roast, about 2½ pounds
  (Black Angus or other branded beef preferred)
3 slices bacon

Sprinkle the rub all over the roast and allow the roast to come to room temperature. Drape the bacon over the top of the meat. Set up your smoker for indirect heat. Use wood chips, chunks, or logs, and keep up a good level of smoke. Maintain a temperature between 275° and 300°F.

Smoke the roast for 1½ to 2 hours, rotating it to expose all sides to the heat. Reposition the bacon as necessary to keep it on top of the roast. Continue cooking, checking and turning every half hour, until the roast reaches an internal temperature of around 135°F for medium-rare. Allow the roast to rest for 15 minutes before slicing. After resting, the roast should reach 140°F. (The USDA recommends 140°F.)

SERVES 6

Rick Schmidt's Shoulder Roast

AT KREUZ MARKET IN LOCKHART, SHOULDER CLOD IS THE MOST POPULAR BEEF cut. "It's a nice cut of beef, so you can serve it a little pink," says pit boss Rick Schmidt. But a whole untrimmed shoulder clod weighs around twenty pounds—a little large for the average home smoker. And the carving is really tricky—the grain goes three different ways. "A shoulder roast is the same cut of meat, and it's an easier size for home barbecuing," Schmidt advises. The only problem is that without all the fat, the meat tends to dry out. That's why I've added the bacon.

1 USDA Choice beef shoulder roast, about 3 pounds
  (Black Angus or other branded beef preferred)
2 teaspoons salt
1 teaspoon cracked black pepper
$1/4$ teaspoon cayenne
3 slices bacon

Let the roast come to room temperature. Combine the salt, pepper, and cayenne and sprinkle the roast with the rub. Drape the roast with the bacon.

Set up your smoker for indirect heat. Use wood chips, chunks, or logs, and keep up a good level of smoke. Maintain a temperature between 300° and 350°F (or as hot as your smoker will allow without charring the meat).

Allow the roast to smoke for 2 hours, rotating to expose all sides to the heat. Reposition the bacon as necessary to keep it on top of the roast. Continue cooking, checking and turning every half hour, until the roast reaches an internal temperature of around 140°F for medium. (The USDA recommends 140°F.) Allow the roast to rest for 15 minutes before slicing.

SERVES 6 TO 8

Jim Goode's "Plugged" Brisket

THIS RECIPE EMPLOYS A VARIATION ON AN OLD TECHNIQUE CALLED LARDING.
Larding involves inserting pieces of fat into the lean part of a roast in order to
improve the tenderness. This used to be done with a tool called a larding needle.
Jim Goode, the founder of Houston's Goode Company Barbecue, does the same
thing with plugs of fat cut from the underside of the brisket. He seasons them and
inserts them into slits cut into the lean meat.

Besides running one of the top barbecue pits in Texas, Jim Goode is also a
former chuck wagon cook-off competitor and an all-around expert on Texas
cookery.

Packer's cut (untrimmed) USDA Select beef brisket, 8 to 10 pounds
3 cloves garlic
1 cup Jim Goode's Beef Rub (page 218)
1 tablespoon olive oil
6 cups Jim Goode's Barbecue Mop (page 219)

On the lean side of the brisket, you'll find some pieces of hard fat. Remove
some with a knife, cut it into $1/4$-slices, and then cut the slices into square plugs
about an inch long. Make about 12 of these plugs. Cut the garlic cloves into thin
slivers.

In a mixing bowl, combine the plugs and garlic slivers with a few tablespoons
of the rub and the olive oil, and turn with a spatula to mix well.

With a paring knife, make 1-inch-deep slits on the lean side of the brisket at
regular intervals. Widen the hole with your finger and force a fat plug and 2 slivers of garlic into it. Force them in deep or they will pop out. Repeat to use up all
the plugs and slivers. Season the brisket with the rest of the dry rub, pressing the
spice mix into the meat. Wrap it up in plastic wrap or a freezer bag and refrigerate
it overnight.

Set up your smoker for indirect heat with a water pan. Use wood chips, chunks,
or logs, and keep up a good level of smoke. Maintain a temperature between 210°
and 250°F. Place the brisket in the smoker, as far from the heat source as possible.
Mop every 30 minutes, rotating the brisket to cook it evenly, keeping the fat-side up
at all times. Add charcoal and/or wood every hour or so to keep the fire burning
evenly. The meat is done when a thermometer reads 185°F at the thick end or when
a probe goes through with little resistance.

SERVES 10 TO 12

Jim Goode's Beef Rub

SERIOUS BARBECUERS HAVE THEIR OWN RUB RECIPE. Jim Goode was nice enough to share his, but you'll want to concoct your own.

$^1/_4$ cup salt, or to taste

$2^1/_2$ tablespoons dark brown sugar

2 tablespoons paprika

2 teaspoons dry mustard

2 teaspoons garlic powder

2 teaspoons onion powder

$1^1/_2$ teaspoons dried basil

1 teaspoon ground bay leaves

$^3/_4$ teaspoon ground coriander

$^3/_4$ teaspoon ground savory

$^3/_4$ teaspoon dried thyme

$^3/_4$ teaspoon ground black pepper

$^3/_4$ teaspoon ground white pepper

$^1/_8$ teaspoon ground cumin

Combine all ingredients in a mixing bowl, then put the mixture in a shaker bottle. It will keep in an airtight container for 3 months.

MAKES 1 CUP

LEGENDS

Jim Goode's Brisket Tips

Timing The rule of thumb for timing a brisket is 1 hour per pound at 250ºF, but you have to add another 15 minutes for every time you open the lid or let the fire go below temperature. Most cooks figure $1^1/_2$ hours per pound to be safe, or 15 hours for a 10-pound brisket.

Yield Once you remove the fat cap and allow for shrinkage, a brisket yields about half of the weight you started with, so a 10-pound brisket should yield around 5 pounds of cooked meat.

Jim Goode's Barbecue Mop

THIS MOP IS SO GOOD, YOU'LL BE TEMPTED TO EAT IT LIKE SOUP. THE combination of butter and bacon makes one of the most flavorful, moisturizing marinades you'll ever taste.

4 cups beef broth

2 bay leaves

1 teaspoon dried oregano

2 tablespoons butter

$^1/_4$ cup chopped onion

$^1/_4$ cup chopped celery

$^1/_4$ cup chopped green pepper

$^1/_4$ cup minced garlic

2 tablespoons Jim Goode's
  Beef Rub (opposite)

$^1/_2$ teaspoon dry
  mustard powder

$^1/_2$ teaspoon salt

$^1/_2$ teaspoon ground white pepper

$^1/_2$ teaspoon ground black pepper

$^1/_4$ teaspoon cayenne

Finely grated zest of 2 lemons

Juice of 2 lemons

2 tablespoons soy sauce

2 tablespoons white wine vinegar

1 tablespoon olive oil

1 tablespoon Asian sesame oil

1 pound thin-sliced bacon,
  finely chopped

Bring the broth to a boil, add the bay leaves and oregano, and reduce the heat to a simmer. Melt the butter in a skillet over medium-high heat and add the onion, celery, green pepper, garlic, beef rub, dry mustard, salt, and black and white peppers, and cayenne. Cook for 5 to 7 minutes, or until the onion wilts. Add the broth, lemon zest and juice, soy sauce, vinegar, and oils. Stir to mix.

Cook the bacon until soft, and add the bacon and drippings to the broth. Simmer until reduced by a quarter, about an hour.

MAKES 6 CUPS

Edgar Black Jr.

BLACK'S BARBECUE

"When I was a kid, a cattleman came over to our house one day. It was during the Depression. We lived out in the country then. My dad was out of work at the time and this cattleman wasn't selling any cattle. So he told my dad that if we would move to Lockhart and run the empty grocery store there, then this guy would give him some cattle. So we moved to Lockhart and took over the store.

"In those days, round steaks, porterhouse, and sirloin were all anybody would buy. Nobody ate ground meat, so you always had the forequarters left over. Nowadays you make chuck

Edgar Black's Overnight Brisket

EDGAR BLACK JR. DOESN'T USE A RUB AND HE doesn't use a mop at Black's Barbecue in Lockhart. "The only seasoning is post oak," he says. He starts a big fire in the old brick smoker at 8 P.M. and lets it burn down through the night. Black estimates the temperature starts at around 300°F and slowly goes down. In the morning, he starts the fire back up and cooks the brisket another three hours or until it is tender. This is a great technique if you want to slow-smoke a brisket but you don't feel like getting up and tending a fire all night.

Salt and ground black pepper to taste
Packer's cut (untrimmed) USDA Select beef brisket,
   8 to 10 pounds

Salt and pepper the brisket and let it come to room temperature.

Set up your smoker for indirect heat with a water pan. (Black's doesn't use a water pan, but in a smaller barbecue smoker it helps prevent flare-ups.) Place the brisket in the smoker. Tend the fire, maintaining a temperature of 300°F for 2 or 3 hours. Then add a good amount of fuel, close the flues down to keep the fire at a slow smolder, and go to bed.

In the morning, restart the fire. (Remove the brisket from the barbecue so that it doesn't get covered with ashes when you add the coals.) When the fire is going, add wood and begin smoking again for another 2 or 3 hours. The meat is done when a thermometer reads 185°F at the thick end or when a probe goes through with little resistance.

SERVES 10 TO 12

Cooper's Cowboy Brisket

AT COOPER'S IN LLANO, THEY BURN MESQUITE down to coals in a separate fireplace and then shovel the hot coals into a pit. Grills are placed about eighteen inches above the coals, and the brisket is cooked over the coals for four hours. Then it's wrapped in aluminum foil and cooked for a few more hours. The pit crew opens the brisket packets as they need them, so your brisket could be cooked anywhere from six to twelve hours. This is George W. Bush's favorite brisket.

The best way to imitate this technique is to grill a brisket over mesquite coals in a barrel-type smoker or a Weber for as long as you can manage to keep it from burning. Then wrap it in foil and finish it over indirect heat or in the oven.

Packer's cut (untrimmed) USDA Select beef brisket,
    8 to 10 pounds
Salt and ground black pepper to taste

Rinse the brisket and pat dry. Sprinkle on both sides with salt and pepper and let it come to room temperature.

Light mesquite chunks in a starter chimney. Burn the wood down to coals. Start a fire in another firebox to keep producing more mesquite coals. Cooking the brisket over the coals for 3 or 4 hours is optimal, but just grill it for as long as you can without burning it. Then wrap the brisket in heavy-duty aluminum foil and continue cooking on the grill or in a roasting pan in a 250°F oven. The meat is done when a thermometer reads 185°F at the thick end or when a probe goes through with little resistance.

SERVES 10 TO 12

roasts and such out of it, but back then you barbecued it. Bone-in forequarter cuts were the most common barbecue meat in Texas. All the meat markets and grocery stores sold it. I was still buying cattle at auction and butchering them myself until the 1950s. But when they started sending cattle up north to be fattened in feed lots, the slaughtering business moved north, too.

"And then you ordered your meat from a packing house instead of cutting it up yourself. So there wasn't any reason to barbecue forequarters anymore. I was the first one around here to start ordering brisket. In the 1950s we raised our price. People thought it was pretty outrageous—we started charging a dollar a pound for barbecue."

Mesquite coals are transferred from a fireplace into these giant pits at Cooper's Old Time Pit Bar-B-Q in Llano.

Bubba Hodges' Egypt Brisket

WRAPPING A BRISKET IN FOIL AFTER SEVERAL HOURS OF SMOKING YIELDS tender brisket with a minimum of work. This is the method used by Bubba Hodges, the pit boss at John's Country Store. He smokes the brisket there with a blend of half mesquite and half pecan for about two and a half hours, basting every thirty minutes with John Northington's mop sauce. The mesquite adds a lot of smoke flavor in a short time. The brisket is then wrapped in aluminum foil with onions and lemons from the mop sauce and cooked in the smoker for several more hours. The result is falling-apart-tender beef with lots of smoke flavor. To order the seasoning mix, see "Online and Mail Order Sources" on page 252.

Packer's cut (untrimmed) USDA Select beef brisket,
   8 to 10 pounds
1 cup Tony Chachere's Original Seasoning
   (or the dry rub of your choice)
6 cups John Northington's Mop (opposite)

    Rinse the brisket and pat dry. Sprinkle it on both sides with the dry rub. Wrap in plastic wrap and refrigerate overnight.

    Set up your smoker for indirect heat with a water pan. Use wood chips, chunks, or logs, and keep up a good level of smoke. Maintain a temperature between 210° and 250°F. Place the brisket in the smoker, as far from the heat source as possible. Mop every 30 minutes, rotating the brisket to cook it evenly, keeping the fat-side up at all times. Add charcoal and/or wood every hour or so to keep the fire burning evenly.

    After 4 hours, wrap the brisket in heavy-duty aluminum foil with what's left of the mop sauce, including the onions and lemons. Seal and continue cooking over low coals for 4 more hours. (Or put it in a roasting pan in a 250°F oven.) The meat is done when a thermometer reads 185°F at the thick end or when a probe goes through with little resistance.

SERVES 10 TO 12

John Northington's Mop

JOHN NORTHINGTON USES A WHOLE bottle of each ingredient. I've cut the proportions down for home barbecuers.

1 cup vegetable oil
$^1/_2$ cup white vinegar
$^1/_2$ cup cider vinegar
1 cup ranch dressing
3 small onions, sliced
one 10-ounce bottle Lone Star beer
3 tablespoons soy sauce
2 lemons, cut in half

Combine all ingredients in a large pot, squeezing the lemons as you add them. Simmer for 30 minutes, or until the onions are soft. Keep the mop sauce in a pot on top of the smoker so it stays hot.

MAKES ABOUT 6 CUPS

LEGENDS

John's Country Store
EGYPT

The screen door slams behind me, and it takes a minute for my eyes to adjust to the darkness inside. At John's Country Store in Egypt, just north of Wharton, there are antique 7-Up signs on the walls and old patent medicines on the shelves. A safe with the inscription "Northington Land Cattle Company 1867" sits on the floor. The windows are just big wooden shutters, hinged at the top and propped open with two-by-fours—no screens, no glass.

At an antique desk, a strange stuffed dummy of an old black woman sits in a long dress and frilly hat. Bubba Hodges, the pit boss, tells me it is the likeness of the paymaster, a woman named Miss Ivory. "That desk is where all the wages were given out on this plantation for over a hundred years."

John's Country Store was called G. H. Northington Sr. Mercantile Store when it first opened in 1900. Over the years, a feed store, meat market, and saloon were added to the original structure, creating the once booming commercial center of Egypt. In 1978, one of G. H. Northington's descendants, John Northington, took over the buildings and changed the name to John's Country Store. He sells beer, barbecue, and antiques on the weekends—sometimes. If the weather is bad, he doesn't bother. It's a barbecue joint in a plantation ghost town.

Harley's Grand Prize Brisket

HARLEY GOERLITZ IS ONE OF THE WINNINGEST BARBECUE COOK-OFF competitors in Texas. He likes to cook an eight- to ten-pound brisket for eight to nine hours on a barrel smoker. He doesn't use a thermometer, but I'd estimate his smoker was running at around 250°F when I watched over his shoulder. Harley makes and sells a dry rub but you can use your own. He mops the meat every hour or so and keeps a water pan with water and onions bubbling away inside the barrel. "Don't add too much wood or you'll oversmoke it," Harley says. He also keeps the fat-side up at all times so the melting fat can baste the meat as it cooks.

Packer's cut (untrimmed) USDA Select beef brisket, 8 to 10 pounds
1 cup Harley's Dry Rub (see Online and Mail Order Sources on page 252),
   or the rub of your choice
2 small onions for the water pan
6 cups mop sauce of your choice
1 stick (¹/₂ cup) butter

    Season the brisket with dry rub, pressing the spice mix into the meat. Wrap it up in plastic wrap or a freezer bag and refrigerate it overnight.

    Cut the onions in half and put them in the water pan. (If your barbecue didn't come with a water pan, use a fireproof steel bowl.) Add water to fill the pan.

    Set up your smoker for indirect heat with a water pan. Use wood chips, chunks, or logs, and keep up a good level of smoke. Maintain a temperature between 210° and 250°F. Place the brisket in the smoker, as far from the heat source as possible. Mop every 30 minutes, rotating the brisket to cook it evenly, keeping the fat-side up at all times. Add charcoal and/or wood every hour or so to keep the fire burning evenly. The meat is done when a thermometer reads 185°F at the thick end or when a probe goes through with little resistance. Melt the butter and generously mop the meat with it just before serving.

SERVES 10 TO 12

Tommy Wimberly's Kilgore Brisket

THE KLASSIC KOOKERS BARBECUE TEAM FROM KILGORE HAS WON TROPHIES around the state. Head cook Tommy Wimberly has an unorthodox approach to brisket cooking. He starts the meat fat-side down to get the fat cap cooking first, then he flips it. And he finishes it wrapped in foil and smothered with barbecue sauce. See "Online and Mail Order Sources" on page 252 for information on ordering Tony Chachere's Original Seasoning.

Packer's cut (untrimmed) USDA Select beef brisket, 8 to 10 pounds
Salt and coarsely ground Malabar black pepper to taste
1 cup Tony Chachere's Original Seasoning
  (or the dry rub of your choice)
1 bottle (18 ounces) Kraft Thick and Spicy Barbecue Sauce
  (or bottled sauce of your choice)

Rinse the brisket and pat dry. Sprinkle on both sides with salt, pepper, and the dry rub. Wrap in plastic wrap and refrigerate overnight.

Set up your smoker for indirect heat with a water pan. Use wood chips, chunks, or logs, and keep up a good level of smoke. Maintain a temperature between 300° and 325°F. Put the brisket in the smoker, fat-side down. After 2^1/$_2$ hours, turn the brisket over and cook it fat-side up for another 2^1/$_2$ hours. Add charcoal and/or wood every hour or so to keep the fire burning evenly. After 5 hours, wrap the brisket in heavy-duty aluminum foil and spread the barbecue sauce all over it. Allow it to cook in the foil on the smoker or in a roasting pan in a 300°F oven for 2 more hours, then hold it in an ice chest for 3 or 4 hours. (Or move it to a 200°F oven.) The meat is done when a thermometer reads 185°F at the thick end or when a probe goes through with little resistance.

SERVES 10 TO 12

Darrington Penitentiary Barbecued Brisket

THIS ISN'T THE WAY BENNY WADE CLEWIS REALLY LIKES HIS BRISKET, BUT AT Darrington Penitentiary he doesn't have any choice in the matter. You can use any mop sauce as a cooking liquid.

$1/4$ cup liquid smoke
4 cups beef broth
2 bay leaves
2 cups chopped onion
2 cups chopped carrot
$1/2$ cup chopped celery
$1/2$ cup chopped green pepper
$1/4$ cup salt
3 tablespoons minced garlic
$1/4$ cup Worcestershire sauce
1 teaspoon ground black pepper
$1/2$ cup cider vinegar
Packer's cut (untrimmed) USDA Select beef brisket, 8 to 10 pounds

Combine all of the ingredients except the beef in a Dutch oven and stir to blend. Add the brisket and enough water to submerge the beef. Allow to marinate overnight in the refrigerator.

Put the Dutch oven on the stove and cook over medium heat until it comes to a boil, turning the brisket so it doesn't burn. Reduce the heat to low and simmer the brisket in the marinade on top of the stove for 1 hour.

Preheat the oven to 350°F. Transfer the brisket to a chopping block and cut it into slices. Put it back into the Dutch oven and cook in the oven for 2 hours, or until very tender.

SERVES 10

Robb's Brisket Disaster Sandwiches

I WANTED TO HAVE A BARBECUE ONE SUNDAY, SO I PUT A BRISKET ON THE smoker at eight on Saturday night and tended the fire carefully until I went to bed at around eleven. I intended to get up and check the fire through the night, but I didn't wake up until four A.M. By then the fire had gone out. The brisket had plenty of smoke flavor, and since I was using the John's Country Store recipe that called for wrapping the brisket in aluminum foil with some mop sauce, I figured I'd just put the wrapped brisket in the oven at 200°F instead of trying to start another fire in the middle of the night.

At five A.M., I was awakened by the smoke alarm. That's how I learned that you can't put a foil-wrapped brisket directly on the oven rack—it punctures the foil and allows the fat to run all over the oven and smoke up the house.

After I cleaned up the oven, I put the foil-wrapped brisket into a roasting pan and put it back in the oven at around six A.M. I went back to sleep. Everything would have worked out fine if I hadn't left the oven on all day. By the time of the barbecue on Sunday night, the brisket was as mushy as *carne guisada*. It tasted good, though.

What do you do with five pounds of squishy, overcooked brisket? You chop up the meat, add a little sauce, and make it into the classic Texas barbecue joint leftover delicacy—chopped beef sandwiches. This recipe also works well for other brisket disasters, such as when you burn the bottom of the brisket. Just cut off the black part and chop up the rest.

Brisket scraps
Barbecue sauce of your choice
Hamburger buns or kaiser rolls

Sliced onions
Sliced pickles

Chop the brisket well, remove any fat, and combine with the barbecue sauce in a mixing bowl to form a "sloppy joe" consistency.

Toast the buns or rolls and spoon a generous helping of the chopped brisket mixture on each. Top with onion and pickle slices.

ON THE
BARBECUE
TRAIL

Following the Smoke

THREE MEN SIT ON THE BENCH in front of Dozier's Grocery on FM 359 in rural Fulshear. I pause on the wood-plank front porch for a minute to read the handwritten notes on the bulletin board. A pick-up truck honks as it passes by. The three men look up and wave. Inside the grocery is a small collection of convenience store items up front and a huge meat market in the back, selling sausage, brisket, and ribs hot off the smoker. This is the way Texas barbecue used to be.

As small-town retail districts fade away, some of the oldest barbecue joints in Texas have closed their doors or moved to greener pastures. Meanwhile, in urban Texas strip malls, new barbecue restaurants are decorated to look like old country stores. The high-school kids who work there probably don't even know why. In these new automated operations, employees load meat onto the racks of gas-fired rotisserie ovens, push a button, and go home. The virtual barbecue oven does the rest. The quality of the smoked meat pales in comparison to the taste of meat cooked the old-fashioned way with nothing but smoke.

Cash register and white bread at
City Market in Luling.

The Business of Barbecue

Whenever I see an unlicensed shade-tree barbecue stand along the side of a Texas farm-to-market road, I think of history's first barbecue salesmen—those famous outlaws, the buccaneers.

In the French West Indies, the word for a barbecue grill is *boucan* (from Tupi, a Brazilian language). *Boucanée* means smoked meat. Hence, "buccaneer" is derived from the French word for "barbecuer." The buccaneers were a ragtag crew consisting mainly of French and English outlaws and escaped slaves. They hid from the Spanish on the island of Tortuga off the northern coast of Hispaniola in the mid-1600s. Although they would later be known for their seafaring exploits, their original business was smoke-cured meat.

The buccaneers hunted the wild cows and pigs left behind by failed Spanish settlements on the island of Hispaniola. They smoke-cured the meat and sold it to passing ships. Hunted themselves by the Spanish, the buccaneers banded together for their own protection. Eventually they gave up on the meat business and went to sea. Soon they discovered that capturing Spanish vessels by surprise attack was a lot more lucrative than chasing wild pigs. Before long, the buccaneers came to be known more as fearless seamen than as barbecue purveyors. But many would argue that it was in their first occupation that they made their most significant contribution to humanity.

Like the buccaneers, Texas barbecue joints are forever at odds with the authorities. Barbecue is, by definition, a primitive cooking process. The health laws in many Texas counties do not allow restaurants to cook outdoors. Many barbecue joints build tin roofs, screened porches, and other elaborate facades to bring the outdoor cooking indoors (at least technically). In outlaw tradition, the best barbecue generally comes from the joint that is in the most trouble with the health department.

These high-tech barbecue ovens do fill a need, though. They make barbecue convenient and consistent. They also solve the building code and air pollution problems that make old-fashioned barbecue pits difficult to build in big cities . . . and they are slowly but surely replacing the real thing.

As Marshall McLuhan observed, "Because we are benumbed by any new technology—we tend to make the old environment more visible; we do so by turning it into an art form and by attaching ourselves to the objects and atmosphere that characterized it."

Old-fashioned Texas barbecue has became an art form. As each old barbecue joint disappears, the ones that remain become more treasured. Here are some barbecue joints that are worth a visit. Most of them are old places. A few are new places that still do things the old-fashioned way. When you're driving around, don't forget to keep your eyes open. You never know when you might happen upon a shade-tree barbecue stand or a little shack that nobody's ever heard of—with the best smoked meat in creation.

Sign in front of Ruthie's Pit
Bar-B-Q in Navasota.

The Barbecue Belt

THE TOWNS OF LOCKHART, TAYLOR, AND ELGIN ARE MAJOR STOPS ON ANY tour of the Central Texas barbecue belt. All three towns are located on rail lines in farm country. The shopping districts of these towns are nearly empty today; buildings stand unoccupied and pedestrians are rare, but in their heyday, these were bustling cotton shipping centers. On a Saturday night during the harvest season fifty years ago, their streets were packed with merchants, farmers, and cotton pickers out for a night on the town.

Lockhart

During the Spring 1999 session of the Texas Legislature, the House of Representatives approved a resolution naming Lockhart the "Barbecue Capital of Texas." Three of the town's barbecue joints were lauded in *Texas Monthly*'s 1997 barbecue survey, and now there's a fourth one: the enormous new location of Kreuz Market. These barbecue joints draw customers from hundreds of miles around.

Black's Barbecue

215 N MAIN STREET,
512-398-2712

Established by Edgar Black Sr. in 1932, during the Great Depression, this landmark's first barbecue pits were located in a tin shed behind the meat market/grocery store across from the current restaurant location. You can eat "1932 style" on butcher paper or work your way through a cafeteria-style serving line that includes various salads and side dishes.

Smitty's Market

208 S COMMERCE STREET,
512-398-9344

This is the original location of Kreuz Market, and the smokers here are more than a hundred years old. Stop by early for some of the best sausage rings in the state. The pork loin is also excellent. Take a tour of the old dining halls, where the knives are chained to the tables. In the days of the cotton pickers, this not only prevented the disappearance of the knives, it also cut down on knife fights.

Kreuz Market

(PRONOUNCED "KRITES")
619 N COLORADO STREET,
512-398-2361

For many years Kreuz was called the best barbecue joint in the state by magazines, newspapers, and barbecue writers. Their smoked meats are still the finest you may ever taste, but since their move to the new location they have lost some of the tradition that made the experience so impressive. The new location is not a meat market, but it continues in the meat market tradition. The beef, sausage, and pork are served on brown butcher paper without barbecue sauce. In a bow to modern times, however, a side dish of beans is now being offered.

Chisholm Trail Bar-B-Q

1323 S COLORADO,
512-398-6027

In 1978, Floyd Wilhelm sold his fishing boat to raise the money to open this place. "Sometimes, I look back and think I must have been crazy," he says. "Starting a barbecue place here was like opening a ballpark across the street from Yankee Stadium." Nevertheless, Chisholm Trail draws a crowd of regulars every day at lunchtime.

Taylor

As the home of the state's most serious competition, the Taylor International Barbecue Cook-Off, Taylor is a barbecue capital in its own right. Two of the state's most historic barbecue joints lie within a couple of blocks of each other in the city's downtown shopping district. The old center of Taylor has been used as a film set and looks like a time capsule from the 1950s.

Louie Mueller Barbeque

206 W 2ND STREET,
512-352-6206
Louie Mueller Barbeque was established in the mid-1940s in a small tin shed in the alley behind Louie Mueller's Complete Food Store. A few years later, Louie opened his second location in south Taylor to accommodate the cotton pickers and farmers who came to town looking for something to eat when they got off work. He moved to the present location in 1959.

The place looks different since they added the new dining room. It was always dark and smoky inside; now the big windows make the place positively cheerful. Mueller's is consistently rated one of the top barbecue restaurants in the state. The brisket is excellent, and so are the pork ribs. If you want to try beef ribs, come early on Saturday. Louie Mueller's has side dishes and sauces as well.

Taylor Cafe

101 N MAIN STREET,
512-352-2828
The Taylor Cafe is a tiny beer joint with two bars—a leftover from the days of segregation. It sits on an all but abandoned block of Main Street that is now shadowed by a highway overpass. In the 1950s, Taylor Cafe was a rough-and-tumble honky-tonk that catered to itinerant agricultural workers and cotton pickers. There was a fight almost every night, remembers owner Vencil Mares. The cotton pickers are gone now and there aren't so many fights anymore, but otherwise the Taylor Cafe hasn't changed an iota in fifty years.

Elgin

Named the "Sausage Capital of Texas" by the 1995 Texas legislature, this little farm town is serious about sausage. Elgin sausage, or "Elgin hot guts" as the old-timers called it, originated at Southside Market, whose original location in downtown Elgin opened in 1886.

Southside Market owner Ernest Bracewell Sr., a former Armour meat salesman, bought the business in 1968. Because the law forbids a company from trademarking a place name, Southside Market was unable to protect the name "Elgin Sausage,"

and as a result, dozens of different companies have sprung up over the years in Elgin, each selling its own version of Elgin sausage.

Southside Market is still the leading producer, with an output of around a million pounds a year. Its logo shows the state of Texas outlined in sausage. If you stretched out a million pounds of sausage, it would actually be enough to accomplish this feat, I'm told.

In the summer, when barbecue season is in full swing, Bryan Bracewell, a grandson of the owner and chief of sausage production, guesses that all together the sausage makers in the town of Elgin turn out around 100,000 pounds of sausage a week. "That would be a conservative estimate," says Bryan.

Southside Market & BBQ

1212 HIGHWAY 290 WEST,
512-281-4650
Founded in 1882 by an itinerant butcher who sold meat door to door, Southside Market is the birthplace of the legendary "Elgin hot guts,"

a fiery hot, natural-casing, all-beef sausage.

After over a hundred years in the old butcher shop at 109 Central Street, the owners were unable to get fire insurance on the old building. The Bracewell family moved the business out to a new building on Highway 290 in 1996. The new location combines a barbecue restaurant with one of the largest sausage-making operations in the state. Southside sells its Elgin sausage both cooked and uncooked at its meat market and also from its Web site. (See "Online and Mail Order Sources" on page 252.)

Meyer's Elgin Smokehouse

188 HIGHWAY 290 EAST, 512-281-3331

The barbecue restaurant is only two years old, but Meyer's Elgin Sausage is a familiar name to Central Texas barbecue fans. The sausage has been available in area grocery stores for many years. While Southside's Elgin Hot Sausage is all beef, Meyer's Elgin Sausage comes in several different flavors. The restaurant serves the all-beef and garlic pork varieties, as well as brisket, turkey, and other smoked meats. You can also have Meyer's Elgin Sausage shipped to your door.

(See "Online and Mail Order Sources" on page 252.)

Crosstown BBQ

211 CENTRAL AVENUE, 512-281-5594

With the big and shiny new sausage emporiums right out on Highway 290, many barbecue hounds miss out on this funky gem nestled in the center of town. It's a dark and seedy little dive—just what a Texas barbecue joint is supposed to look like. Crosstown makes their own all-beef sausage (this is Elgin, after all). But it's their greasy mutton, tender brisket, and chewy pork ribs that are the real attractions.

Ten Old Meat Markets and Grocery Stores

IF YOU'RE GOING TO TAKE A TREK OUT TO THE OLD MEAT MARKETS, REMEMBER that they eat lunch early in farm country. Consider skipping breakfast and showing up at 11 A.M. to get first choice of the day's best cuts. By 12:30, any small-town barbecue joint worth its salt has sold out of its most popular items, and they aren't open for dinner.

City Market (Luling)

633 E DAVIS, NEAR US HIGHWAY 183, LULING 210-875-9019

"We don't have any forks," the cashier at City Market repeats emphatically every five minutes. Visitors who aren't familiar with Central Texas barbecue traditions are dumbfounded by the lack of eating utensils. Why do we eat barbecue with our hands?

Because that's the way cotton pickers did it, that's the way the oil-field workers did it, and that's the way it's done.

Open since 1930, Luling's City Market is an old meat market that hasn't changed much since the Depression. Try the juicy brisket and the sausage; they have two kinds, wet and dry. The wet one squirts when you cut it.

Prause's Market

253 WEST TRAVIS STREET (HIGHWAY 71), LA GRANGE 409-968-3259

Prause's may not have the best smoked meat in the state, but it's a great place to see how the Texas barbecue joint evolved. The same family has run Prause's for more than a hundred years, and it's been in its present location since 1952. It's still more of a meat market than a barbecue joint—like a butcher shop with a lunch room. Be sure and come early; the sausage links and brisket always sell out.

City Meat Market (Giddings)

101 W AUSTIN, GIDDINGS
409-542-2740
There's always some brisket and sausage for lunch at City Market in Giddings, but get there early because owner and pit boss Gerald Birkelbach doesn't cook all day. This is another meat market that sidelines in barbecue. They do custom butchering, too, in case you want a special cut. It's a great place to get your deer processed.

City Market (Shulenburg)

HIGHWAY 77, 3 MILES
NORTH OF SHULENBURG
979-743-3440
The "best little meat market in Texas" makes some outrageous jalapeño sausage. Quite a bit of it goes to the Salt Lick Steak House restaurant chain, but you can buy some, too, if you get here early. There are a couple of booths for barbecue customers in front of the meat case, although the offerings are usually limited to brisket sandwiches and hot sausage. Their smoked pork loin is very popular around Christmastime. You slice it up and eat it cold. Don't forget to buy some dry sausage to eat in the car.

Dozier's Grocery

FM 359, FULSHEAR
281-346-1411
The crispy ribs, tender brisket, and house-made garlic sausage, jalapeño sausage, and German sausage at this grocery store rank among the best in the state. The sauce is good, too, but you don't need any. Established in 1957, Dozier's is the closest meat-market barbecue joint to downtown Houston. (It's 28 miles from 610 West to Fulshear.) George Bush Sr. used to fly Dozier's pecan-smoked bacon to Washington on *Air Force One*.

John's Country Store

EGYPT
979-677-3536
This rambling wreck of a country store with meat market and old-fashioned saloon attached was established in 1900 as G. H. Northington's store. The place is really more of a historical curiosity than a barbecue joint. Brisket sandwiches are all they serve (unless potato chips count). Be sure to call first—they sometimes open only on weekends. It is a very popular place to rent for big corporate events and family reunion barbecues.

Gonzales Food Market

311 ST. LAWRENCE STREET, GONZALES
830-672-3156
800-269-5342
The Lopez family has been selling barbecue out of their grocery store in downtown Gonzales since 1959. Ray

Lopez is the pit boss, and his beef ribs are the best I've ever had. (See Ray Lopez's Beef Ribs, page 195.) The brisket is also melt-in-your-mouth tender. Gonzales is the home of the "Come and Take It" cannon—you can see the tiny artillery piece that started the war with Mexico in the state historical museum down the street.

Novosad's Meat Market

105 LA GRANGE STREET, HALLETSVILLE
361-798-2770
This is one of the old Czech barbecue joints where cold canned peaches are a favorite side dish. The menu has been updated by third-generation owners Nathan and Laura Novosad. Unusual cuts like lamb ribs and pork steaks are popular here. They've also brought house-made beans, cole slaw, cucumber salad, fresh-baked bread, and other pleasant (though untraditional) touches to the old meat market.

Market Bar-B-Que and Fresh Meats (Smolik's)

208 E CALVERT, KARNES CITY
830-780-3841
Soft drinks and meats by the pound, fresh or smoked, are the only things offered at this old-time butcher shop and barbecue. William Smolik founded the place in 1918, according to family legend, and it has remained in the same location throughout its history. William's son, George Smolik, sold the place to the

current owners in 1992. The Smolik family continues to use the family name at other meat markets around the state, including the Smolik's in Cuero, which is famous for its homemade Czech sausage.

Austin's Barbecue

EAGLE LAKE
979-234-5250
The former filling station has no charm; it's just the barbecue outlet for the old Austin's Grocery Store next door, which was established in 1950. The house sausage is outstanding—you can buy some next door to cook at home—and the brisket is usually pretty good, too. Get a couple of pounds to go and skip the tomato-heavy barbecue sauce.

Ten in the City

THERE ARE SOME THREE THOUSAND BARBECUE PURVEYORS IN THE STATE OF Texas, and nobody will ever sample all of them. Here is some of the best big-city barbecue I've tried.

Sonny Bryan's Smokehouse

2202 INWOOD ROAD, DALLAS, 214-357-7120
The late Sonny Bryan had a devoted following. *New York Times* food and politics writer R. W. Apple Jr. was not the only food lover to declare Sonny Bryan's the best in Texas. Sonny Bryan's original location, a little drive-in-style restaurant on Inwood, is the sentimental favorite. There are picnic tables outside and a little room in front where you can eat at old school desks. The meats you eat at Sonny Bryan's are not fresh from the smoker. They are smoked in advance, refrigerated, and then reheated on the grill. The ribs come out very tender and falling off the bone, which is probably why the rib sandwich is so popular here.

North Main Barbecue

406 N MAIN STREET, EULESS
817-283-0884
If it looks like a trucking company, you've got the right place. The guys who run North Main Barbecue are actually in the trucking business. They are also members of a barbecue cook-off team. The team won so many trophies that they decided to start selling barbecue at the trucking company on Fridays and Saturdays. Stop by on a weekend for a brisket sandwich or an all-you-can-eat platter. Don't miss the pork ribs—you'll notice they've won an awful lot of trophies for them.

Angelo's Barbecue

2533 WHITE SETTLEMENT ROAD, FORT WORTH
817-332-0357
The stuffed black bear that greets you at the door sets the tone. Decorated with moose heads and fishing trophies, Angelo's looks like a big, dark hunting lodge. Angelo's brisket is among the best in the state. It is smoky, perfectly seasoned, and so tender you could cut it with a pickle spear. But it's Angelo's cold beer that people in Fort Worth talk about. The beer schooners at Angelo's are made of thick glass and are kept in a huge freezer at an extremely low temperature. When a draft beer is first poured into the glass, the beer freezes along the sides.

Railhead Smokehouse

2900 MONTGOMERY STREET, FORT WORTH, 817-738-9808
As the new kids in town, the folks at the Railhead will be the first to admit that they learned everything they know from Angelo's. Like Angelo's, the Railhead has excellent brisket and tender ribs, but the population of Fort Worth seems to be divided on the subject of which one has colder beer. Traditionalists favor the dark interior of Angelo's, while the younger set gravitates toward the picnic tables outside at the Railhead. The next time you find yourself in Fort Worth, I suggest you try them both.

Drexler's Bar-B-Que

2020 DOWLING STREET,
HOUSTON, 713-752-0008

Harry Green built this old cinder-block pit on Houston's East Side in 1952. James Drexler carries on the proud tradition that has been handed down from his uncle. Don't miss the falling-off-the-bone East Texas ribs, tender brisket, and definitive East Texas beef links. This is the best East Texas–style barbecue in Houston.

Williams Smoke House

5903 WHEATLEY, HOUSTON
713-680-8409

This little cabin in the pines feels like it's way out in the country when in fact it's only a short drive from downtown. Sit under trees at a picnic table if the weather's nice. The oak- and pecan-smoked brisket is excellent, and so are the East Texas ribs and beef links.

Goode Company

5109 KIRBY, HOUSTON
713-522-2530
WWW.GOODECOMPANY.COM

Jim Goode was a chuck wagon cook-off competitor and barbecue buff who decided to go into business. His original restaurant on Kirby is one of the best of the new breed of Texas barbecue joints. The brisket, pork roast, and ribs are excellent. There are two choices of sausage—jalapeño and Czech.

Sam's

2000 E 12TH STREET,
AUSTIN, 512-478-0378

This old wooden house still has a rusty screen door and an out-house behind the woodpile. Sam's was a favorite of the late Stevie Ray Vaughan and many other blues musicians. Sam's is still very popular with the out-all-night crowd—it's open very late. Try the ribs and the sausage.

Stubb's

801 RED RIVER, AUSTIN
512-321-7719

The late C. B. Stubblefield was a legend in Lubbock. He not only fed up-and-coming musicians like Terry Allen and Joe Ely, he also showed up at their sets and jammed with them. Stubb's barbecue restaurant on Red River in Austin is a music venue, bar, and restaurant. The ribs and chicken here are amazing, but the brisket is hit or miss. The Sunday Barbecue and Gospel Music Brunch is absolutely fabulous.

Tom's Ribs

13323 NACOGDOCHES ROAD,
SAN ANTONIO, 210-654-7427
CONTACT@TOMSRIBS.COM

This hugely popular rib joint also serves brisket and smoked turkey along with a full menu of sides dishes. Baby back ribs are the specialty of the house. San Antonio–born Tom Norris moonlighted at several restaurants while he was a crew member aboard the U.S.S. *Thrush* stationed in Miami. He went on to open several barbecue joints in Florida before returning home. The Tom's Ribs location on Nacogdoches is the original family restaurant, several other locations have been opened with partners in San Antonio and more are planned.

LEGENDS

All in the Family

The Mikeska family is the Lone Star State's widest-ranging barbecue dynasty. All of the Mikeska restaurants are cafeteria-style operations with pretty good barbecue and outrageous hunting trophies. The Mikeskas all also have huge catering operations.

Rudy Mikeska's
300 W 2nd Street, Taylor
800-962-5706

Maurice Mikeska's
218 Merchant Street and
4225 Highway 59, El Campo
800-388-2552
www.mikeskabbq.com

Jerry Mikeska's
Interstate 10 East, Columbus
800-524-7613

Clem Mikeska's
1217 S 57th Street, Temple
800-344-4699

And a Few for the Road

LIKE MOST TEXAS FOOD LOVERS, I PLAN MY CAR TRIPS AROUND THE OPENING and closing times of interesting barbecue spots. These are a few of my favorite "road trip" stopovers.

Cooper's Old Time Pit Bar-B-Q

604 W YOUNG (HIGHWAY 29), LLANO
915-247-5713

No Hill Country tour is complete without a stop at Cooper's, George W. Bush's favorite barbecue joint. They cook cowboy-style over mesquite coals, and you order your meat straight from the pit and pay for it inside. The sirloin and pork chops are awesome if you get them at the perfect time. (See Lorenzo Vences' Sirloin, page 144.) The brisket is also excellent. The barbecue sauce here is bolstered with brisket juices and is truly outstanding.

Joe Cotten's

HIGHWAY 77 SOUTH, ROBSTOWN (CORPUS CHRISTI)
512-767-9973

The highway that most people take to South Padre Island, Port Isabel, and the Lower Rio Grande Valley goes right by Joe Cotten's front door. Generations of Texans have come to associate the place with a trip to the beach, but Cotten's gained its fame during the heyday of offshore drilling. It's said that all the big oil deals of that era were sealed here. The mesquite-smoked brisket sausage and ribs are all top notch. The distinctive barbecue sauce

tastes like Mexican salsa ranchera. (See Barbecued Tomato Salsa, page 90.)

Harry's on the Loop

FM 1323 (OFF HIGHWAY 16 NEAR FREDRICKSBURG)
210-685-3553

During bluebonnet season in April, this may be the prettiest drive in Texas, but you'd better hit Harry's early because the barbecue sells out fast. The pork ribs are fabulous and the brisket is pretty good, too—if there's any left. The picnic tables outside are my favorite, but the inside of the old house is also fun. Be sure to sign one of the walls, and see if you can find Eric Clapton's autograph while you're at it.

New Zion Missionary Baptist Church Barbecue

2601 MONTGOMERY ROAD, HUNTSVILLE
409-295-7394

When driving between Houston and Dallas, the best place to stop for lunch is the combination Baptist Church hall and barbecue joint that's been called the "Church of the Holy Smoke," where you sit and eat family-style at community tables. Don't miss the tender East Texas–style ribs and brisket, but skip the commercial sausage. Above all, save room for the wonderful homemade sides.

(See Huntsville Butter Beans, page 128, and Mashed Potato Salad, page 126.)

Ruthie's Pit Bar-B-Q

905 W WASHINGTON (HIGHWAY 105 WEST), NAVASOTA
409-825-2700

There is a big apiary in Navasota, and I met some of my beekeeper friends here for lunch. Ruthie's son, Louis Charles Henley, is the jocular pit boss at this ramshackle East Texas–style joint. His ribs are excellent, his Elgin sausage is smoked for several hours until it gets really dense, and his pork shoulder is sublime. (See Ruthie's Pork Shoulder, page 119.) The restaurant is an old house—you can pick a magazine from the rack while you wait for your meal. Mutton ribs are served on Saturday afternoon, but you'll be lucky to get any—there's a waiting list for them.

Leon's "World's Finest" In & Out B-B-Q House

55TH AND BROADWAY, GALVESTON
409-744-0070

This is a good place to grab some ribs to go for lunch on the beach, but if you want to sample some awesome sides, sit down at one of the eight tables. (See the recipes for

Leon O'Neal's Turnip Greens and Green Beans, page 129, and Leon's Stepped-Up Rice, page 130.) The potato salad is the best you'll ever have at a barbecue joint.

Charlie's Bar-B-Que

110 MAIN STREET,
SMITHVILLE
512-547-3481

My daughters Katie and Julia love this stopover in quirky Smithville between Austin and Houston. Pork shoulder, ribs, mutton, and excellent pork and beef sausage are the best things to order at Charlie's. The brisket has a habit of drying out before you get there. But the real reason to go is to experience the time warp of Smithville's Main Street and sit around in the old dining room under the lazy ceiling fans and discuss the weather with hard-working gimme cap and over-all–clad Texans.

Salt Lick

FM 1826, DRIFTWOOD
512-858-4959

The Salt Lick features cowboy-style open pit barbecue and a very interesting Asian-style barbecue sauce concocted by founder Thurmond Roberts' Hawaiian wife, Hisako Roberts. When I was a student at the University of Texas, the Salt Lick used to have an all-you-can-eat, family-style special for six or more people. These days my friends are more interested in the garden walk and country setting than in seeing how many ribs they can eat, but going out to the Salt Lick

is still one of my favorite Sunday drives.

Clark's Outpost

101 HIGHWAY 377, TIOGA
940-437-5529

People drive for hours to eat the famous barbecue at Clark's Outpost in the tiny town of Tioga, north of Denton. It's not on the way to anywhere. The tender brisket is smoked for several days, and the ribs are excellent. The side dishes and desserts are a little overwhelming here if you're used to the simple offerings at the old meat markets. There are green salads, baked potatoes, French fries, and corn on the cob, among many other vegetables. There are also elaborate desserts like bread pudding and Dutch apple pie.

Lum's Bar-B-Que

2031 N MAIN STREET,
JUNCTION
915-446-3541

On the way out to Big Bend, we usually stop in Junction for a rib plate or a brisket sandwich at Lum's. It's a grocery store with a few tables inside and a really lovely picnic area outside. They smoke their meat cowboy-style over mesquite. Rumor has it that they used to have smoked *cabrito* ribs, but I've never seen any. They do have enticing-looking cream pies, though.

Buster's BBQ

303 RR 620 N, LAKE TRAVIS
(OUTSIDE OF AUSTIN)
512-266-3926

My brother Scott keeps his

sailboat out on Lake Travis. That's where you'll find Buster's, home of Buster's H-Bomb (page 160), "the best sandwich in Central Texas" according to John Kelso of the *Austin American-Statesman*. It's made with slices of pork shoulder that each have a bull's-eye of garlic and jalapeño in the middle.

Johnny's Barbecue

703 W FERGUSON STREET,
PHARR
956-787-9263

We usually end our vacations to South Padre Island on Sunday. We leave in the morning to start the long drive home. But first, we swing by Johnny's in Pharr for breakfast. Johnny's is basically an old Lower Rio Grande Valley beer joint that serves barbecue, but on Sunday morning they have some spectacular *barbacoa*.

Ray's Roundup and Quick Stop

HIGHWAY 281,
ORANGE GROVE
361-384-3025

On the trip from South Padre to points north, Johnny's *barbacoa* breakfast keeps us going until about noon—and right about that time, we're driving by Ray's Roundup and QuickStop, on 281 north of Falfurrias. Ray Esquival's smoker sits right out by the highway; when you see smoke, stop in and get a brisket sandwich and a cold beer. Ray flavors his excellent barbecue sauce with hot brisket drippings. (See page 74.)

A BARBECUE GLOSSARY

Achiote Paste

Achiote paste is made from ground annatto seeds, which come from a tropical tree of the same name. Sometimes the paste is a combination of the ground seeds and other spices. It is a favorite seasoning throughout Mexico, especially in the Yucatán. Annatto seeds turn foods a bright orange. In fact, they are used to color Cheddar cheese.

According to many cookbooks, you can grind annatto seeds in a coffee grinder to make your own achiote paste. I haven't had any luck with this. Annatto seeds are so hard that after ten minutes of grinding, I seldom get more than a little dust. I've heard that soaking the seeds in water overnight helps. However, I suggest that you forget about making achiote paste and buy it already made at a Mexican market.

Beans

Whether you're cooking pinto beans, butter beans, or any other variety, you have probably heard a lot of different opinions on how it should be done. Some people recommend that you soak beans overnight and change the water to aid digestibility. Most Mexican cooks insist that adding salt to the beans before they're done makes them tough. How much truth is there to any of this?

In an article in the *Los Angeles Times*, food editor Russ Parsons challenged these old nuggets of wisdom.

According to Parsons, his own independent testing revealed that presoaking the beans didn't aid digestibility, but it did hurt the flavor and texture. He also said that salting the water while the beans were cooking had no effect on tenderness but did improve the taste.

According to the bean scientists at the California Dried Bean Advisory Board, if you presoak dried beans and then change the water, you make them more digestible by eliminating some of the oligosaccharides that leach into the water during soaking. The Bean Board is curiously mum about the salt, but it claims that acids such as those present in tomatoes, chiles, and vinegar will slow the tenderizing process, so these ingredients should be added after the beans are cooked.

The debate between these two points of view reveals that cooking is still more of a subjective art than an exact science. Russ Parsons' article also points out that the more often you eat beans, the easier it is for your digestive system to adjust to them. Soaking may remove oligosaccharides, but veteran bean eaters like Russ Parsons obviously don't have any problems with oligosaccharides (whatever they are) anyway.

In my opinion, the first and most important thing to remember about the digestibility of beans is that you have to cook them until they're done. It's amazing how often people get impatient and eat the beans before they're ready. As for the salt, I thank Russ Parsons for finally proving what I always suspected—that adding the salt doesn't make any difference in the tenderness of the beans. And if it does take an extra couple of minutes for salted beans or beans with tomatoes or chiles added to soften, well, what's a couple of minutes to a pot of beans?

The biggest factor in the tenderness of beans isn't what you add to them, it's the age of the beans you're cooking. Old beans take longer to cook, and the skin is always tougher.

Barbacoa

Just as the word "barbecue" has many meanings in English, the world *barbacoa* has many meanings in Spanish. In Central Mexico, *barbacoa* is lamb or goat meat wrapped in maguey leaves and roasted or steamed on hot coals. In Texas, Mexican ranch hands adapted this interior Mexican style of *barbacoa* to roast cattle heads, or *cabezas*. They wrapped the *cabezas* in maguey leaves or later aluminum foil and canvas and buried them in earthen pits with hot coals. As the years went by and the practice of burying the *cabezas* came to be outlawed by the health authorities, the heads were roasted and steamed in ovens.

In the Tejano tradition, the term *barbacoa* has come to mean the meat from the head of a steer, regardless how it is cooked.

Black Pepper

Almost every barbecue rub calls for black pepper. Some cook-off competitors swear by whole Malabar black peppercorns, freshly ground or cracked. Others favor peppercorns from Tellicherry and Lampong. Using cracked pepper in a rub gives the meat a distinctive flavor.

Cracked pepper is very different from freshly ground pepper. The aroma and flavor of the peppercorn come through in every bite.

To make cracked pepper, you need to crush each peppercorn into no more than eight or ten pieces. You can put whole peppercorns in a large frying pan and use a smaller frying pan to crush them, but you really need to bear down hard and this takes a lot of strength.

The easiest cracking method is to put the peppercorns in a food processor and pulse it once or twice. This method takes patience and usually requires several batches. You have to sort through the cracked peppercorns, remove the remaining whole peppercorns, and repeat the process. The simplest way to keep cracked peppercorns is to buy a bottle of whole black peppercorns, crack them all, and then return them to the same bottle for storage.

Búfalo Chipotle Sauce

Búfalo is a Mexican brand of hot sauce made with chipotle peppers and tomatoes. It's sort of like a chipotle ketchup. If you can't find it, purée a chipotle pepper and add ketchup until you like the flavor, or make the Chipotle Ketchup (page 88). But be forewarned, chipotles are very hot.

Chickens

The recipes in this book were tested with commercial fryers. You can substitute free-range chickens or roasting hens if you want, but the cooking times will be longer. Since the skin on a barbecued chicken tends to get too dark anyway, you may want to wrap a larger chicken in aluminum foil when it reaches the desired color.

Chile Peppers

We often use the words "chiles" and "peppers" interchangeably in the Southwest, but we often use them together, too. One reason for the popularity of the redundant term "chile peppers" is that the words "chili" and "chile" refer to specific dishes in Texas and New Mexico. "Chili" means chili con carne, but it is actually an alternate spelling of "chile" and is pronounced the same in English. Texas writer and naturalist J. Frank Dobie used the "chili" spelling to refer to both the peppers and the dish. Pepper expert Dr. Jean Andrews, author of *Peppers: The Domesticated Capsicums*, advocates the English spelling, "chilli."

Dallas columnist Frank X. Tolbert, who started the Terlingua chili cook-off, fought a humorous war with New Mexico over the spelling of the word. "Chile" in New Mexico means a pepper, but it also means green chile stew. "Chile pepper" may be a redundant term, but the redundancy is often necessary to make it clear that you are talking about the pods and not a specific dish.

FRESH CHILES Fresh chile peppers are usually harvested in the green stage. Fully ripened red chiles are most often used for drying, but they also sometimes turn up fresh in the supermarket. Green or red chiles can be used interchangeably unless the recipe specifies one or the other. The following fresh chile peppers, listed from mildest to hottest, appear in this book:

Anaheim Also known as the long green chile by New Mexicans (until it turns red and becomes the long red chile), the Anaheim has a pleasant vegetable flavor and ranges from slightly warm to medium-hot on the heat scale. Anaheims are generally roasted and peeled before they are used. The name comes from a chile cannery that was opened in Anaheim, California, in 1900 by a farmer named Emilio Ortega. Since Ortega brought the pepper seeds to California from New Mexico, most New Mexicans feel the name is a misnomer. I call them Anaheims because outside of New Mexico, when you ask for a long green chile at the grocery store, there is no telling what you'll get.

Jalapeño Hot, green, and bullet-shaped, the jalapeño is the classic Tex-Mex hot pepper and one of the world's best-known chiles. Originally grown in Mexico, it is named for Jalapa, a town in the state of Veracruz. The fresh jalapeño has a strong, vegetal flavor to go with the heat. I prefer to cook with fresh jalapeños, but the jalapeño is most widely consumed in its pickled form. Along with barbecue sauce, pickles, and raw onions, pickled jalapeños are a popular condiment in Texas barbecue joints.

Serrano Similar to the jalapeño, the serrano is hotter and smaller. Most Mexicans claim that serranos have a fuller, more herbaceous flavor. Since the vast majority of jalapeños are pickled, the serrano is actually the most widely used fresh chile pepper in Texas.

Pequín Also known as piquin, chilipiquin, or chiltepin, this tiny chile grows wild throughout southern Texas and northern Mexico. Although " pequín" seems to be a corruption of the Spanish *pequeño*, meaning "small," the Spanish name itself is probably a corruption of *chiltecpin*, a Nahuatl word meaning "flea chile," a reference to both its size and sting. Since these peppers were spread by birds rather than cultivation, experts tell us that pequíns are the oldest chiles in North America. In northern Mexico, they are collected in the wild and sold in markets, where they fetch more than almost any other kind of chile. They are sometimes dried and preserved for year-round use. A pequín bush can be found in almost any backyard or vacant lot in South Texas, and pequíns are therefore very common in home cooking. Because they are not grown commercially, they are seldom found in restaurant cooking or in grocery stores. If you find some, you can

substitute three or four fresh pequíns for one serrano or half a jalapeño.

Roasting Peppers
To roast a fresh pepper, place the whole pepper over a high gas flame and turn it as needed to blister the skin on all sides. Don't allow the flame to burn too long in one place or you'll burn through the pepper. After most of the skin has been well blistered, wrap the warm pepper in a wet paper towel and set it aside to steam gently. When you remove the towel, most of the skin should come off with it. Scrape off the rest of the skin with a butter knife.

If you don't have a gas range, put the pepper in a skillet with 2 tablespoons vegetable oil and blister it over high heat on an electric burner. Then wrap it in a wet paper towel and proceed as directed.

DRIED CHILES The following dried chile peppers can be used for recipes in this book:

Ancho The dried form of the poblano chile, the ancho is very dark brown and wide. (In fact, the word *ancho* is Spanish for "wide.") Anchos are the fleshiest of the dried chiles, and their pulp combines a slightly bitter flavor with a sweetness reminiscent of raisins. They are usually mild, although occasionally one will surprise you with its heat.

Guajillo Tapered with a smooth, shiny, reddish skin, the guajillo has a tart and medium-hot flavor. Dried anaheims are also sometimes called guajillos, but they are much milder. This pepper makes an excellent chile powder, and it can also be substituted for, or added to, ancho peppers in barbecue sauce.

Pasilla Long and skinny with a black, slightly wrinkled skin, the pasilla has a strong, satisfying bitter flavor and can range from medium-hot to hot. The name comes from the Spanish, *pasa*, meaning "raisin," a reference to the appearance of the skin. This makes an excellent chile powder, and it can also be substituted for, or added to, ancho peppers in barbecue sauce.

Chipotle The chipotle is a smoke-dried jalapeño. Small, wrinkled, and light brown chipotles have an incredibly rich, smoky flavor, and they are usually very hot. Smoking as a method of preserving jalapeños was already common in Mexico when the Spanish first arrived. The original Nahuatl spelling, *chilpotle*, is also sometimes seen.

To make chipotle chile powder, you need to use dried chipotles, but canned chipotles are acceptable in sauce recipes. Canned chipotles have been soaked in some kind of sauce, usually a vinegary adobo sauce. There is no need to soak canned chipotles, just stem and seed them and purée them with some of the sauce from the can.

Chili Powder and Chile Powder

Several of the recipes in this book call for chili powder, while others call for chile powder. These are two different things. Chili powder is sold in most grocery stores; it contains ground chile peppers along with cumin and other spices. It was invented by the Gebhart Company in San Antonio in the late 1800s.

Chile powder is made of pure ground chile peppers. Paprika is a chile powder made of mild sweet peppers. You can buy other chile powders at some gourmet or ethnic stores, or you can make them at home in an electric coffee grinder. Making your own chile powders allows you to use such flavorful peppers as chipotles, guajillos, and pasillas in your cooking. Select brittle dried peppers for this purpose, or put pliant dried peppers into a 350°F oven for 10 minutes to dry them out.

Clean all the coffee out of the grinder. (You may want to grind a little salt or cornmeal to get the rest of the coffee out.) Stem and seed the pepper, and cut it into pieces small enough to fit easily into the grinder. Grind the pepper for a minute or so until it yields a fine powder. I keep several bottles of chile powder on my spice rack, labeled by variety.

If you decide to make chile powder at home, remember to clean the pepper out of the grinder, or you'll have some very interesting coffee the next morning.

Soaking and Puréeing Dried Chiles There's not much to it. Just put the dried chiles in a bowl with enough hot water to cover them. Put a saucer or an upside-down coffee mug on top to keep the peppers submerged. Leave them there until they are soft. This usually takes from 15 to 30 minutes. Chipotles are very hard and tend to take longer. You can speed up the process by simmering them gently in water on the stovetop.

If you're making a chile purée for a barbecue sauce, you want the peppers very soft, so you can leave them in the water longer. When they are soft enough, pull the stems off and scoop out the seeds. Put the flesh in the blender with enough of the soaking water to get the blades turning. Purée until smooth. Chile peppers vary in size, so you'll have to estimate how much purée you'll get by checking the size of the peppers. Anchos yield the most purée, guajillos and other shiny-skinned peppers yield very little. When selecting peppers to make a purée, use the softest, most pliable ones available.

You can boost the flavor of the purée a little by soaking the peppers in stock instead of hot water. If you're making a sauce for brisket, use beef stock. Chicken stock is good for chicken and pork.

Handling Chile Peppers

It's wise to wear rubber gloves when handling jalapeños and serranos. Get a little juice from the cut-up pepper on your face or in your eyes and you can count on ten minutes of sheer agony. If you don't have rubber gloves, use a piece of plastic wrap to hold the pepper while you cut it. Clean the knife and the cutting board immediately with hot soapy water. If your hands get into the pepper juice,

try soaking them for a few minutes in a mild bleach solution.

Hog Casings

Because so many Texans make venison sausage, you can find medium hog casings in most Texas grocery stores during deer season. But even if you don't live in Texas, natural sausage casings aren't that hard to find. Ask your butcher, or look in the yellow pages under "Butcher's Supplies."

You need about 10 feet of casings for 5 pounds of sausage, but you'll probably have to buy a lot more than that. The casings come packed in salt in a plastic tub. But don't worry if you have more than you need; they keep forever.

Hot-Pepper Sauce

Some of the recipes in this book specify Tabasco sauce as an ingredient. Others call for Louisiana or habanero hot-pepper sauce. What we mean by hot-pepper sauce is a solution of vinegar or other liquids in which pepper solids and flavorings are suspended. This kind of sauce comes in a shaker bottle. Chunky salsas and picante sauces are not the same thing.

Louisiana is famous for its pepper sauces. So is Mexico. Some are much hotter than others. Habanero pepper sauces tend to be incendiary. You can use the pepper sauces interchangeably, thereby making your food as hot as you like it.

MSG

If you want to be a barbecue judge, you'd better not be too sensitive to this stuff. Monosodium glutamate, aka MSG, is one reason that so many cook-off competitors like to keep their recipes secret. Nobody likes to admit that the barbecue rub is spiked with MSG because the flavor enchancer has gotten such a bad name. But the truth is, the stuff really does make things taste better, and if I were trying to win a barbecue cook-off I would use it, too. Barbecue joints, on the other hand, have had to stop using MSG because so many people complain about it. It's used in many commercial rubs and barbecue sauces, so check the ingredient list carefully if you want to avoid it.

Mexican Oregano

Mexican oregano is a member of the verbena family and is very different from Mediterranean oregano. It can be found dried in Mexican markets and some supermarkets, but it is sometimes difficult to find fresh. Planting a little in your garden is the best guarantee of having some on hand.

Rice

Long-grain white rice will work fine, but we much prefer the new long grain—a basmati hybrid called Texmati. It is aromatic and retains a nutty firmness when cooked. Basmati is an excellent substitute.

Salt

Table salt (sodium chloride) is mined salt with additives to keep it free-flowing, often combined with iodine (sodium iodide) in areas where the diet is deficient in this important mineral.

Kosher salt is an additive-free coarse mined salt that is often used in meat curing. Sea salt is made by a more costly evaporative process from sea water. Sea salt has become the salt preferred by many gourmets because of its flavor. It will work fine in most of the recipes in this book. However, I have found that kosher salt is preferred by barbecuers for many meat recipes and that the finer, additive-free pickling salt is superior for brining solutions and canning.

Smoked Tomatoes

While you have your barbecue going, I highly recommend that you get into the habit of smoking a few tomatoes. Smoked tomatoes are the secret of truly great sauces and salsas. Generally, you can place tomatoes on the barbecue for half an hour, but smoking times will vary. Roma tomatoes tend to take longer. Tender summer tomatoes will not take long at all. Substitute the smoked tomatoes for fresh tomatoes in guacamole, pico de gallo, or any recipe that calls for tomatoes.

Tomatillos

Husk-covered tomatillos, which are tart and nearly always cooked before eating, are widely available in grocery stores: look for firm, unblemished tomatillos with tight husks. Many Mexican cooks say that the smaller tomatillos are more flavorful.

Tortillas

Many grocery stores stock a wide variety of tortillas these days. There are plain and flavored flour tortillas, fluffy white corn tortillas, and old-fashioned corn tortillas. The old-fashioned corn ones, sometimes called enchilada tortillas, are the most common. They are very thin and somewhat leathery but hold up well in cooking. Save these for frying—use the flour tortillas and fluffy white corn tortillas for serving at the table: corn with *barbacoa* and *lengua*, flour for sausage wraps and brisket tacos.

Heating Tortillas

Store-bought flour or corn tortillas need to be heated before serving. The easiest method is to wrap them in foil and stick them in a 350°F oven for five to ten minutes. Corn tortillas can also be wrapped in a clean dish towel that has been slightly dampened and put into the oven. The moisture from the towel will steam them slightly and improve their texture as they warm up.

When you need only a few flour tortillas, it's even easier to put a few into an ungreased skillet over medium heat and to flip them quickly as they warm, shuffling the tortillas until each side has been in contact with the skillet for ten seconds or so.

ONLINE AND MAIL ORDER SOURCES

Barbecue

Lots of Texas barbecue restaurants cater major events all over the country. Just contact the restaurant of your choice. Some will also ship small amounts of heat-and-serve barbecue by overnight delivery service. Here are a few you can try.

The Salt Lick

(DRIFTWOOD)

Hisako's famous Asian-style barbecue sauce, as well as ribs, brisket, and sausage, can be ordered from the Web site. *www.salt lickbbq.com, 512-858-4959.*

City Market

(SCHULENBURG)

"The best little meat market in Texas" ships smoked brisket and their famous jalapeño sausage, as well as ready-to-eat snacks like dry jerky-style sausage and peppered pork tenderloin by overnight express. *www.citymarketsch.com, 800-793-3440.*

County Line Barbecue

(10 LOCATIONS)

The County Line is a very successful barbecue restaurant chain with locations in Austin, San Antonio, Houston, El Paso, and Albuquerque. Their restaurants are very clean and attractive, and their barbecue is generally very good, too. *Call them at 800-AIR-RIBS for an overnight delivery. www.air ribs.com.*

Black's Barbecue

(LOCKHART)

Black's ships their awesome pork ribs and other barbecue items by overnight delivery. *512-398-2712*

Cooper's Old Time Pit Bar-B-Que

(LLANO)

President George W. Bush's favorite barbecue joint ships brisket, chicken, ribs, pork chops, plus all kinds of smoked sausages, jerkies, and ham. Ask for a catalog. *www.coopersbbq.com, 877-533-5553.*

Elgin Sausage

There's nothing quite like Texas barbecue sausage, and it ships pretty well. Once you try it, you'll be back for more.

Southside Market

They can ship you their famous sausage already smoked, ready to reheat along with their summer sausages, hot sauce, and barbecue sauce. They also sell gift boxes. *www.southsidemktbbq.city search.com, 512-281-4650.*

Meyer's Elgin Sausage

Choose from these flavors: plain, garlic, sage, beef, or hot. *800-677-6465.*

Dry Rubs and Sauces

Harley's Texas Style Bar-B-Que Seasoning

The winningest cook-off competitor in Texas sells his own dry rub—with or without MSG. *Route 3, Box 781 Giddings, TX 78942. 979-542-3281 or 800-573-9070.*

Adams Rubs

Adams makes an excellent brisket rub that contains plenty of salt, pepper, and spices and the natural meat tenderizer papain, but no MSG.
Adams Extract Co.
P.O. Box 17008, Austin, TX 78760. www.adams extract.com, 512-282-1100.

Adkins Western Style Barbecue Seasoning

A favorite North Texas blend. They also sell gift packs of various seasoning mixes.
American Spice
4560 Mint Way, Dallas, TX 75236. 800-356-2914.

Tony Chachere's Original Seasoning

For a dry rub on brisket and chicken, lots of barbecue cook-off competitors swear by this stuff. *www.tonychachere.com.*

Tex Joy Bar-B-Q Seasoning

The favorite dry rub at New Zion Missionary Baptist Church Barbecue and many other Texas barbecue joints.
www.texjoy.com,
800-259-3400.

Stubb's Bar-B-Q Sauce

Although the master, C. B. Stubblefield, has passed on, his legend lives on in this sauce worthy of its namesake.
512-480-0203.

Canyon's Texas Barbecue Sauce

Winner of the Texas State Fair, this is an excellent sauce. They also sell a grilling and dipping sauce called All Fired Up that adds some pepper and orange flavors.
Canyon Specialty Foods
www.canyonspecialtyfoods.com,
214-352-1771.

Wood

American Wood Products

They'll send you pecan, oak, hickory, mesquite, alder, cherry, or apple wood cut to your choice of barbecue sizes.
800-223-9046.

Barbecue Stores

Goode Company Barbecue

(HOUSTON)
Goode Company's Hall of Flame is a complete barbecue store that carries all kinds of rubs, sauces, and barbecue accessories, as well as barbecue pits and seasoned hardwoods. Call for a catalog.
Hall of Flame,
5015 Kirby, Houston, TX 77098.
www.goodecompany.com,
800-627-3502.

Pitt's & Spitt's

They make a great barbecue sauce and an excellent all-purpose rub, if you don't mind a little MSG. They also sell the best barbecue pits in Texas. Pitt's & Spitt's is also the only place I know of that sells Neox gloves for handling barbecue.
Pitt's & Spitt's
14221 Eastex Freeway
Houston, TX 77032,
www.pittsandspitts.com,
800-521-2947.

Barbecues Galore

These guys have 136 stores in the United States and Australia, and they sell a wide variety of rubs, sauces, barbecue pits, and accessories. You can also order almost anything they sell from their Web site.
www.bbqgalore.com.

Beef Heads for Barbacoa

If your grocery store or meat market can't get you a *cabeza de res* for *barbacoa*, you can call Sam Kane in Corpus Christi and arrange a shipment.

Sam Kane Beef Processors

9001 Leopard, Corpus Christi, TX 78409. 316-241-5000.

TEXAS BARBECUE COOK-OFF CALENDAR

WANT TO VISIT A BARBECUE COOK-OFF? THINKING OF becoming a judge? Or are you ready to go for a trophy? Here's a list of some of the barbecue cook-offs held in the state of Texas every year. The sponsoring association, if any, is listed in parentheses.

Many of the smaller cook-offs, such as the Go Texan county cook-offs, are qualifying events for the larger cook-offs. Winners receive sponsorships that help them defray the costs of competing at the higher levels.

You'll find more information on smaller barbecue cook-offs as well as general barbecue news at these Web sites:
http://texana.texascooking.com
www.ribman.com
www.barbecuenews.com

January

HOLD 'EM & HIT 'EM
FARM & RANCH COOK-OFF,
Houston.
Contact: 281-463-7331 (IBCA).

CYFAIR GO TEXAN
CHILI BBQ COOK-OFF,
Trader's Village, Eldridge
Parkway, Houston. The largest
of the Go Texan Cookoffs.
Contact: 281-376-4817,
or e-mail shelty246@mind
spring.com.

LONE STAR
BARBECUE SOCIETY
COOK-OFF,
Tres Rios RV Park,
Glen Rose.
Contact: 817-261-9507
(LSBS) or e-mail
nichl@airmail.net.

SAN ANTONIO LIVESTOCK
EXHIBITORS' MESQUITE
COUNTRY BBQ COOK-OFF,
San Antonio.
Contact: 210-242-7179.

February

GRIMES COUNTY AREA GO
TEXAN BBQ COOK-OFF,
Navasota.
Contact: 936-825-2020.

HOUSTON LIVESTOCK SHOW &
RODEO WORLD'S CHAMPIONSHIP
BAR-B-QUE CONTEST,
Houston. Reliant Park
(formerly Houston Astrodome)
Parking Area.
Contact: 713-794-9550, or
visit www.rodeohouston.com.

"CHILLY" BBQ &
CHILI COOK-OFF,
VFW 8787, Austin.
Contact: 512-365-7821
or 512-836-8767.

IRVING ELKS LODGE
BBQ COOK-OFF,
Irving.
Contact: 972-579-0005.

March

WEST VOLUNTEER FIRE
DEPARTMENT BBQ COOK-OFF,
West.
Contact: 254-826-3570.

CYPRESS CREEK
EMS BBQ COOK-OFF,
Sam Houston Race Track,
Houston.
Contact: 281-397-7844.

ANDERSON COUNTY
BBQ COOK-OFF,
GO TEXAN'S RICHEST,
Palestine.
Contact: 903-729-5454.

AMERICAN CANCER RELAY
FOR LIFE BBQ COOK-OFF,
Sour Lake.
Contact: 409-287-3171
(IBCA).

AMERICAN LEGION BBQ
COOK-OFF,
Clifton.
Contact: 254-675-3915.

MONTGOMERY COUNTY
BARBECUE COOK-OFF,
Conroe.
Contact: P.O. Box 869, Conroe,
TX 77305.

STAR OF TEXAS RODEO
BBQ COOK-OFF,
9100 Decker Lake Road,
Austin, TX 78724.
Contact: 512-919-3000, or
visit www.staroftexas.org.

April

ALL LITTLE THINGS
COUNT BBQ COOK-OFF,
Bobby's on the Bayou,
Houston.
Contact: 281-580-5076.

SHRINER'S BENEFIT
BBQ COOK-OFF,
Fairgrounds, Baytown.
Contact: 281-437-1157
(TGCBCA).

TERRELL HERITAGE
JUBILEE & BBQ COOK-OFF,
Terrell.
Contact: 972-524-5703, fax
972-563-2363, or 972-524-
5703 (IBCA).

SPRING TURKEY HUNT
BARBECUE COOK-OFF,
DeLeon.
Contact: DeLeon Chamber of
Commerce, 100 S Texas,
DeLeon, TX 76444, 254-893-
2083 (LSBS).

KURTEN COMMUNITY
COOK-OFF,
Kurten.
Contact: 979-778-3279
or 979-589-3113 (IBCA).

40 & 8 AMERICAN LEGION
COOK-OFF,
Willis.
Contact: 936-344-6586
(TGCBCA).

FUNFEST & BBQ COOK-OFF,
Troy. (2nd Cook-Off of the 1st
Half Quad-Cities +1).
Contact: 254-938-7468
(CTBA).

CLEBURNE SPRINGFEST
BBQ COOK-OFF,
Cleburne.
Contact: 817-641-3138 or
817-556-5010, ext. 5010
(IBCA).

BARBECUE COOK-OFF,
Cameron.
Contact: Chamber of
Commerce, 254-697-4979
(CTBA).

VFW POST 8200 BARBECUE
COOK-OFF,
Liberty Hill.
Contact: 512-260-0986
(CTBA).

WICHITA FALLS EAST VFD
BBQ COOK-OFF,
Wichita Falls.
Contact: 940-733-2576
(LSBS).

MILLS COUNTY CABRITO
COOK-OFF,
Goldthwaite.
Contact: Chamber of
Commerce, 915-648-3619
(LSBS).

CHILDREN'S KIDNEY
FOUNDATION BBQ,
Bobby's on the Bayou.
Contact: 713-656-8635
(IBCA).

May

KENDLETON VFD BBQ,
King Park, Kendleton.
Contact: 979-532-8143
(TGCBCA).

VFW 4458 CHILI &
BBQ JAMBOREE,
Caldwell.
Contact: 979-272-3301
(TGCBCA).

TOMBALL AREA SHRINERS
BBQ COOK-OFF,
Bobby's on the Bayou,
Houston.
Contact: 281-350-9111 or
888-765-3866 (IBCA).

FRONTIER DAYS
BBQ COOK-OFF,
Breckenridge.
Contact: 254-559-2301,
or e-mail patsy@chamberof
commerce.com (IBCA).

HIGHLAND LAKES CHILI POD
& BBQ COOK-OFF,
Marble Falls.
Contact: 830-693-5502
(CTBA).

FARMERS MUTUAL
PROTECTIVE ASSOCIATION
OF TEXAS BARBECUE
COOK-OFF,
Belton.
Contact: 254-773-1575 or
254-780-1906 (CTBA).

ELECTRA GOAT COOK-OFF,
Electra.
Contact: Electra Chamber of
Commerce, 112 West
Cleveland, Electra, TX 76360,
940-475-3577 (LSBS).

GRAPEVINE ELKS
LODGE BBQ COOK-OFF,
Grapevine.
Contact: 817-577-9895
(IBCA).

BRUCEVILLE-EDDY
MAYFEST BBQ COOK-OFF
(3rd Cook-Off of the 1st Half
Quad-Cities+1), Eddy.
Contact: 254-859-5874
(CTBA).

TGCBCA INVITATIONAL
BBQ COOK-OFF,
Bobby's on the Bayou,
Houston.
Contact: Sandy Babcock,
281-356-6244 (TGCBCA).

LEE COUNTY FAIR CHARCOAL
CHALLENGE,
Giddings.
Contact: 979-366-2489
(IBCA).

GROESBECK BARBECUE
COOK-OFF,
Groesbeck.
Contact: 254-729-3291
(LSBS).

ABILENE ADULT DAY
OUTHOUSE RACE, BEAN &
BBQ COOK-OFF,
Abilene.
Contact: 915-691-9268
(IBCA).

RIBOLYMPICS,
at Heartland Mall,
US 183 & US 67/US 377,
Early.
Contact: 915-646-8531
(LSBS).

BRADY WORLD
CHAMPIONSHIP
GOAT COOK-OFF
(Memorial Day weekend),
Brady.
Contact: Brady Chamber of
Commerce, 915- 597-3491.

June

FREESTONE COUNTY
BENEFIT BBQ COOK-OFF,
Teague.
Contact: 254-739-2549 or
254-379-3116 (IBCA).

WILD HORSE PRAIRIE DAYS
BARBECUE COOK-OFF,
City Park, West US 380,
Haskell.
Contact: 940-864-3523
(LSBS).

COTTON FESTIVAL
COOK-OFF
(4th Cook-Off of the 1st Half
Quad-Cities +1), Buckholts.
Contact: 254-593-4175 after
8 P.M. (CTBA).

SNOOK FEST BBQ COOK-OFF,
Snook City Park, Snook.
Contact: 979-272-8655
(IBCA).

DUBLIN CHAMBER OF
COMMERCE AND
DR. PEPPER DAYS
BARBECUE COOK-OFF,
City Park, Dublin.
Contact: Dublin Chamber of
Commerce, 218 N Blackjack,
Dublin, TX 76446,
800-938-2546 (LSBS).

AMERICAN LEGION 447
BBQ COOK-OFF,
Round Rock.
Contact: Post 447,
512-244-0480 (CTBA).

ROGERS ROUND-UP
BARBECUE COOK-OFF,
Rogers.
Contact: 254-642-3884
(CTBA).

TEXAS SUMMER
FEST/BALLOON CLASSIC BBQ
COOK-OFF,
Great Southwest Equestrian
Center, Houston.
Contact: 281-414-7263
(IBCA).

FFA BOOSTER CLUB
BARBECUE COOK-OFF,
Burleson County Fairgrounds,
Caldwell.
Contact: Rte. #2, Box 211,
Caldwell, TX 77836,
409-272-8358 (LSBS).

CHISHOLM TRAIL BLAZER
BBQ COOK-OFF,
Fort Worth Stockyards,
Fort Worth.
Contact: 817-625-7005 or
817-485-8785.

WORLD CHAMPIONSHIP OF
TEXAS BBQ COOK-OFF,
Temple.
Contact: 254-298-5415
(CTBA).

ITASCA CHAMBER OF
COMMERCE BBQ COOK-OFF,
Itasca.
Contact 254-687-2331
(IBCA).

July

KIFARU FOR KIDS
BBQ COOK-OFF,
Lampasas.
Contact: 512-556-3838
(CTBA).

CHARITY BAR-B-QUE
COOK-OFF,
Hella Temple,
2121 Rowlett Road, Garland.
Contact: 1158 Highway 78
South, Farmersville, TX
75442, 972-784-7231
(LSBS).

MOULTON TOWN & COUNTRY
JAMBOREE BBQ COOK-OFF,
Moulton.
Contact: P.O. Box 482,
Moulton, TX 77975-0482,
361-596-4034 or 361-596-
7205, fax 361-596-4384, or
e-mail moultontexas@gvec.net
(TGCBCA).

August

TAYLOR INTERNATIONAL
BARBECUE COOK-OFF
(winners qualify for the
American Royal Barbecue
Cook-Off in Kansas City),
Taylor.
Contact: Tim Banichek,
512-365-5717,
512-328-2300, ext. 2343, or
512-352-6364.

HOOF EN' HAIR BARBECUE
COOK-OFF.
Fort Richardson State Park,
Jacksboro.
Contact: 940-567-3506
(LSBS).

NATIONAL CHAMPIONSHIP
BARBECUE COOK-OFF,
Meridian. (By invitation only,
but call or write for details.)
Contact: P.O. Box 699,
Meridian, TX 76665, 254-
435-6113, or e-mail
bbq@htcomp.net (LSBS).

September

WAYLON'S WEST TEXAS
BBQ COOK-OFF,
Littlefield.
Contact: 806-385-5178
(IBCA).

HILL COUNTY AREA GO
TEXAN BBQ COOK-OFF,
Hillsboro.
Contact: 254-576-2992
(IBCA).

FIRE ANT FESTIVAL
BARBECUE COOK-OFF,
Montague.
Contact: P.O. Box 75,
Montague, TX 76251, 940-
894-2391 (LSBS).

CROSSROAD CHAMPIONSHIP
BBQ COOK-OFF,
Victoria.
Contact: 361-572-9454
(TGCBCA).

WILD WEST FESTIVAL
BBQ COOK-OFF,
Springtown.
Contact: 817-220-6462
(IBCA).

CTBA BARBECUE COOK-OFF,
Bartlett.
Contact: 254-527-4430 or
254-527-3898 (CTBA).

HIDDEN COVE PARK BBQ
COOK-OFF,
The Colony.
Contact: 972-294-1443
(IBCA).

MCLENNAN COUNTY GO
TEXAN BBQ COOK-OFF,
Cameron Park, Waco.
Contact: 254-859-5064
(CTBA).

COMANCHE COUNTY
POW-WOW AND BARNIE
MCBEE MEMORIAL
BRISKET COOK-OFF,
City Park, Comanche.
Contact: Comanche Chamber
of Commerce, P.O. Box 65,
Comanche, TX 76442, 915-
356-3233 (LSBS).

HEARNE CHAMBER OF
COMMERCE AND
ROBERTSON COUNTY
GO TEXAN COOK-OFF &
SUNFLOWER FESTIVAL,
Robertson County Fairgrounds,
Hearne (LSBS).
Contact: 979-279-2351

October

KERR COUNTY FAIR
BAR-B-QUE COOK-OFF,
Hill Country Youth Exhibit
Center, Highway 27 East,
Kerrville.
Contact: P.O. Box 290842,
Kerrville, TX 78029-0842,
830-257-6833, or visit
www.kerrcountyfair.com
(CTBA).

TYNAN REC. CLUB
FESTIVAL & BBQ,
Tynan.
Contact: 361-547-8061
(IBCA).

OCTOBERFEST &
BARBECUE COOK-OFF,
City Park, Rising Star.
Contact: Chamber of
Commerce, P.O. Box 189,
Rising Star, TX 76471, 254-
643-2811 (LSBS).

TRADER'S VILLAGE
BBQ COOK-OFF,
Grand Prairie.
Contact: 972-647-2331
(IBCA).

OGLETREE GAP FOLKLIFE
FESTIVAL & BARBECUE
COOK-OFF,
Copperas Cove.
Contact: 254-547-6968
(LSBS).

HARRIS COUNTY FAIR,
FARM & RANCH CLUB
BBQ COOK-OFF,
Houston.
Contact: 281-463-6650
(TGCBCA).

EDDY METHODIST CHURCH
BBQ COOK-OFF,
Eddy, Texas.
Contact: 254-859-5208
(CTBA).

November

CENTRAL TEXAS
BARBECUE ASSOCIATION
BBQ COOK-OFF,
Flag Hall SPJST Lodge 25,
Cyclone (CTBA).
Contact 254-778-1756,
or e-mail jbiles@vvm.com

WORLD CHAMPIONSHIP
WILD HOG COOK-OFF
ON THE SQUARE
Crowell.
Contact: Crowell Chamber
of Commerce, P.O. Box 79,
Crowell, TX 79227, 940-684-
1670 (LSBS).

Barbecue Associations

Texas barbecue cook-off participants keep track of upcoming events, who's winning what, changes in the rules, and general gossip through their regional barbecue associations. Several of these groups have newsletters that they can send you for more information about barbecue cook-offs in your area.

Central Texas Barbecue Association (CTBA),
3401 LAS MORAS,
TEMPLE, TX 76502
Contact: 254-778-1756,
or e-mail jbiles@vvm.com.

Cowtown Barbecue Association,
FORT WORTH, TX.
Contact: Henry Erwin,
817-457-0599.

East Texas Barbecue Cookers Association (ETBCA),
2709 CEDARCREST,
MARSHALL, TX 75670.
Contact: doncdt@tiac.net.

International Barbecue Cookers Association (IBCA),
P.O. BOX 300556,
ARLINGTON, TX 76007-0556.
Contact: 817-469-1579,
or e-mail ibcalynn@aol.com.
Web site www.ibcabbq.org.

Lone Star Barbecue Society (LSBS),
P.O. BOX 120771,
ARLINGTON, TX 76012.
Contact: 817-261-9507, fax 817-795-1968, or e-mail nich1@airmail.net.

Texas BBQ Association,
7540 CIRCLE DRIVE,
RICHLAND HILLS, TX 76180.
Contact: 817-485-8785,
or e-mail llb63@msn.com.

Texas Gulf Coast Barbeque Cookers Association (TGCBCA),
26611 WEIR WAY,
MAGNOLIA, TX 77355.
Contact: 281-356-6244.

West Texas Barbecue Association (WTBA),
9413 WEST UNIVERSITY,
P.O. BOX 5615, ODESSA, TX 79764.
Contact: 915-366-7227.

National Barbecue Association,
P.O. BOX 9685,
KANSAS CITY, MO 64134.
Contact: 888-909-2121,
or e-mail nbbqa@nbbqa.org.

BIBLIOGRAPHY

Aidells, Bruce and Dennis Kelly. *The Complete Meat Cookbook*. New York: Houghton Mifflin, 1998.

Andrews, Jean. *Peppers: The Domesticated Capsicums*. Austin: University of Texas Press, 1984.

Bayless, Rick. *Authentic Mexican*. New York: Morrow, 1987.

Caro, Robert A. *The Path to Power*. New York: Vintage, 1981.

Cusik, Heidi Haughy. *Soul and Spice: African Cooking in the Americas*. San Francisco: Chronicle Books, 1995.

Dearden, Patrick. *A Cowboy of the Pecos*. Plano, Texas: Republic of Texas Press, 1997.

Dobie, J. Frank. *A Vaquero of the Brush Country*. New York: Grosset and Dunlap, 1999, (originally published by Southwest Press, 1929).

Ellis, Merle. *Cutting Up in the Kitchen: A Butcher's Guide to Saving Money on Meat and Poultry*. San Francisco: Chronicle Books, 1975.

Ferber, Edna. *Giant*. New York: Doubleday, 1952.

Flemmons, Jerry. *More Texas Siftings*. Fort Worth: Texas Christian University Press, 1997.

Foley, Neil. *White Scourge: Mexicans, Blacks and Poor Whites in Texas Cotton Culture*. Berkeley: University of California Press, 1999.

Kafka, Barbara. *Roasting*. New York: Morrow, 1995.

Linck, Ernestine Sewell. *Eats: A Folk History of Texas Food*. Fort Worth: Texas Christian University Press, 1992.

Luchetti, Cathy. *Home on the Range: A Culinary History of the American West*. New York: Villard, 1993.

Price, Byron B. *National Cowboy Hall of Fame Chuck Wagon Cookbook*. New York: Hearst Books, 1995.

Thorne, John. *Serious Pig*. New York: North Point Press, 1996.

Online Sources

The Handbook of Texas Online:
    www.tsha.utexas.edu/handbook/online

FSA/OWI Transcripts: American Memory Collections, Library of Congress:
    http://memory.loc.gov/ammem

Photo Credits

©BETTMANN/CORBIS: 178-179

LBJ Library, Robert Knudsen: 143

LBJ Library, Yoichi Okamoto: 35, 138

Library of Congress, FSA-OWI Collection, Dorothea Lange: 155

Library of Congress, FSA-OWI Collection, Russell Lee: 4-5, 76-77, 112-113, 152-153

Wyatt McSpadden: 27, 70-71, 94-95, 188-189, 233

Michael Murphy: 13-19

Deron Neblett: 174-175

Texas State Library, Archives Division: 2-3, 20-21, 30-31, 32

University of Texas, Arlington, Fort Worth Star-Telegram Collection: 134-135

The UT Institute of Texan Cultures, no. 84-484, Courtesy of Margaret Virginia Crain Lowery: 24-25,

The UT Institute of Texan Cultures, no. 80-516, Courtesy of the Estate of Roger Fleming: 28

The UT Institute of Texan Cultures, no. 76-388, Courtesy of Mrs. Stacy Labaj: 98-99

The UT Institute of Texan Cultures, no. 96-384, Courtesy of Pat S. Woods: 106

The UT Institute of Texan Cultures, no. 3042-D, The San Antonio Light Collection: 200-201

The UT Institute of Texan Cultures, no. 3042-F, The San Antonio Light Collection: Cover, 137

The UT Institute of Texan Cultures, no. 4-26-1990 F, The San Antonio Express-News Collection: 173

Scott Van Osdol: 36-37

Will Van Overbeek: 12-13

Robb Walsh: 15, 42-43, 54-55, 57-58, 62-64, 80, 103, 115, 118, 122-123, 127, 158, 164-165, 184-185, 195,
197, 208-209, 213, 235, Back cover

INDEX

Table of Equivalents

The exact equivalents in the following tables have been rounded for convenience.

Liquid/Dry Measures

U.S.	Metric
1/4 TEASPOON	1.25 MILLILITERS
1/2 TEASPOON	2.5 MILLILITERS
1 TEASPOON	5 MILLILITERS
1 TABLESPOON (3 TEASPOONS)	15 MILLILITERS
1 FLUID OUNCE (2 TABLESPOONS)	30 MILLILITERS
1/4 CUP	60 MILLILITERS
1/3 CUP	80 MILLILITERS
1/2 CUP	120 MILLILITERS
1 CUP	240 MILLILITERS
1 PINT (2 CUPS)	480 MILLILITERS
1 QUART (4 CUPS, 32 OUNCES)	960 MILLILITERS
1 GALLON (4 QUARTS)	3.84 LITERS
1 OUNCE (BY WEIGHT)	28 GRAMS
1 POUND	454 GRAMS
2.2 POUNDS	1 KILOGRAM

Length

U.S.	Metric
1/8 INCH	3 MILLIMETERS
1/4 INCH	6 MILLIMETERS
1/2 INCH	12 MILLIMETERS
1 INCH	2.5 CENTIMETERS

Oven Temperature

Fahrenheit	Celsius	Gas
250	120	1/2
275	140	1
300	150	2
325	160	3
350	180	4
375	190	5
400	200	6
425	220	7
450	230	8
475	240	9
500	260	10